MOUNT ST. HELENS

IMAGES OF AN UNEXPECTED LANDSCAPE

MOUNT ST. HELENS

IMAGES OF AN UNEXPECTED LANDSCAPE

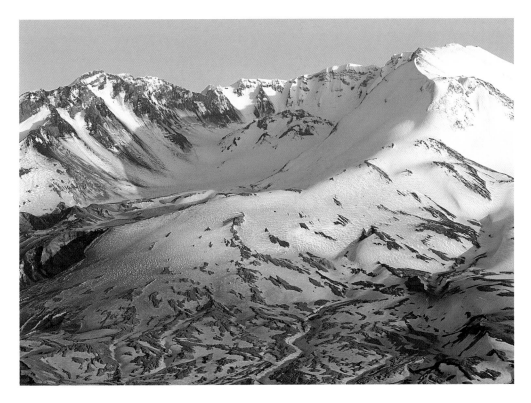

MARK LEMBERSKY

FOREWORD BY SENATOR MARK HATFIELD

BLUE HERON PUBLISHING

Cover/book design and typography: Elizabeth Watson
Map: Marge Mueller

Published by SoftLight Ink, an imprint of Blue Heron Publishing
1234 SW Stark Street, Portland, Oregon 97205
Telephone: 503-221-6841, Facsimile: 503-221-6843
E-mail: publisher@blueheronpublishing.com

First Edition, 2000
9 8 7 6 5 4 3 2 1

ISBN 0-936085-48-7

Printed in Singapore

Photos: *Front Cover, Mount St. Helens two decades after the 1980 eruption;
Page 5: Shattered trees and renewed growth near Spirit Lake; Page 6: Flourishing
plant life just five miles due north of the volcano; Page 8: Daybreak.*

ACKNOWLEDGMENTS

This book grew from a combination of Phil Wikelund's ideas,
encouragement by former Monument Manager Gloria Brown,
the receptiveness of publisher Dennis Stovall, and the bringing
together of all of us by dedicated friend Robyn Andersen.
Senator Mark Hatfield graciously agreed to write the Foreword
about his personal experiences and Ursula Le Guin generously
contributed the use of her poem. Betty Watson designed the book
and suggested the title; I am delighted with the results and it is
a great pleasure to work with her. Marge Mueller produced the
informative map in record time. Rae Nelson gave me innovative
ideas and fresh perspectives at critical times.

This book would not be possible without all of their help
and support, for which I am truly grateful.

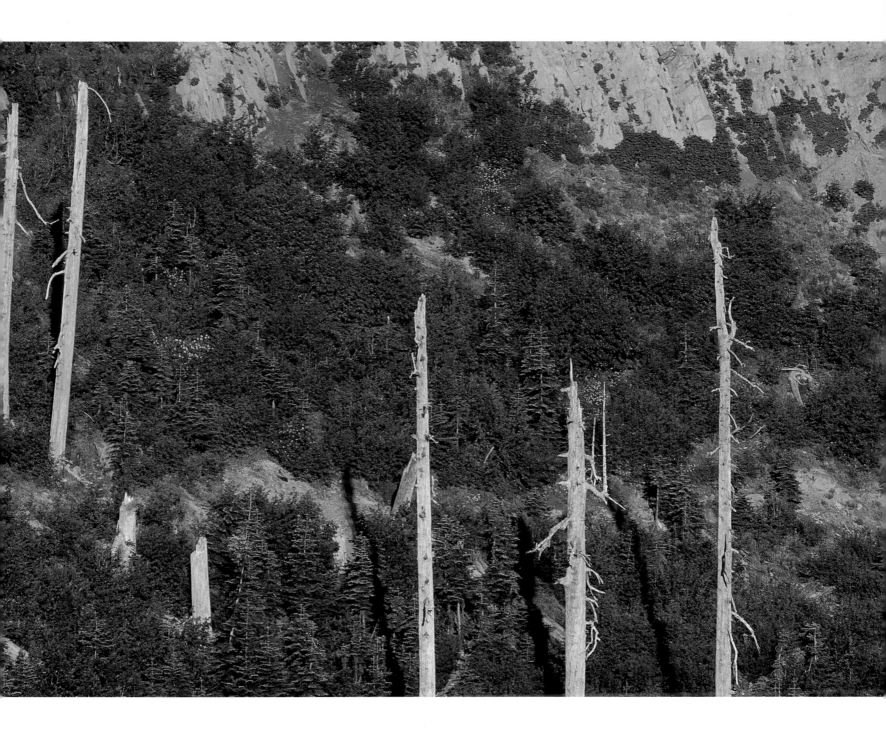

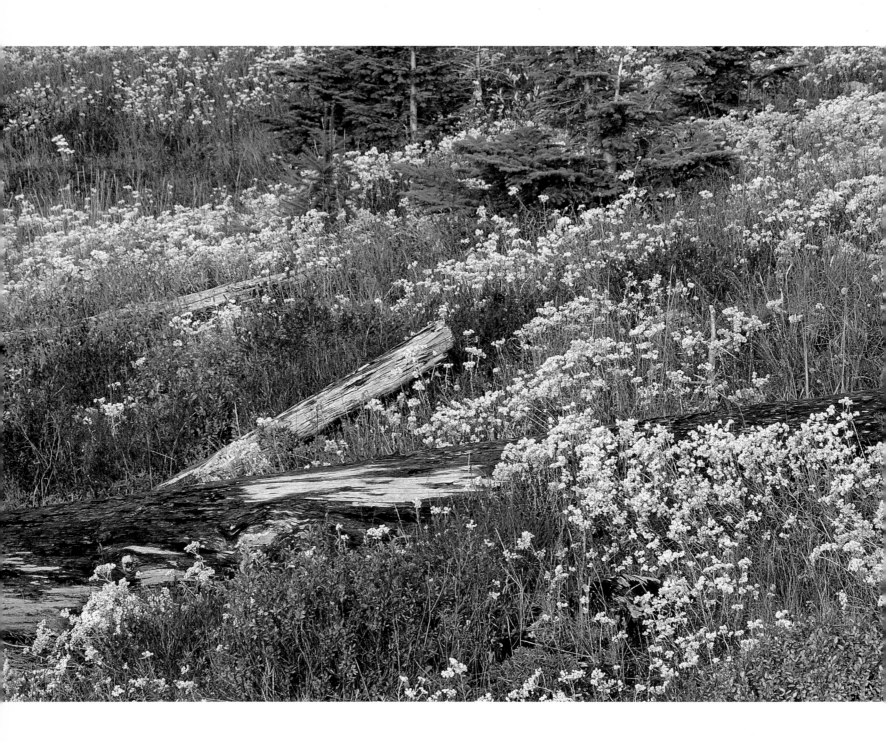

DEDICATION

To my Mother *Alice* and Father Herman,

in appreciation of their sacrifices willingly made to open doors for me.

CONTENTS

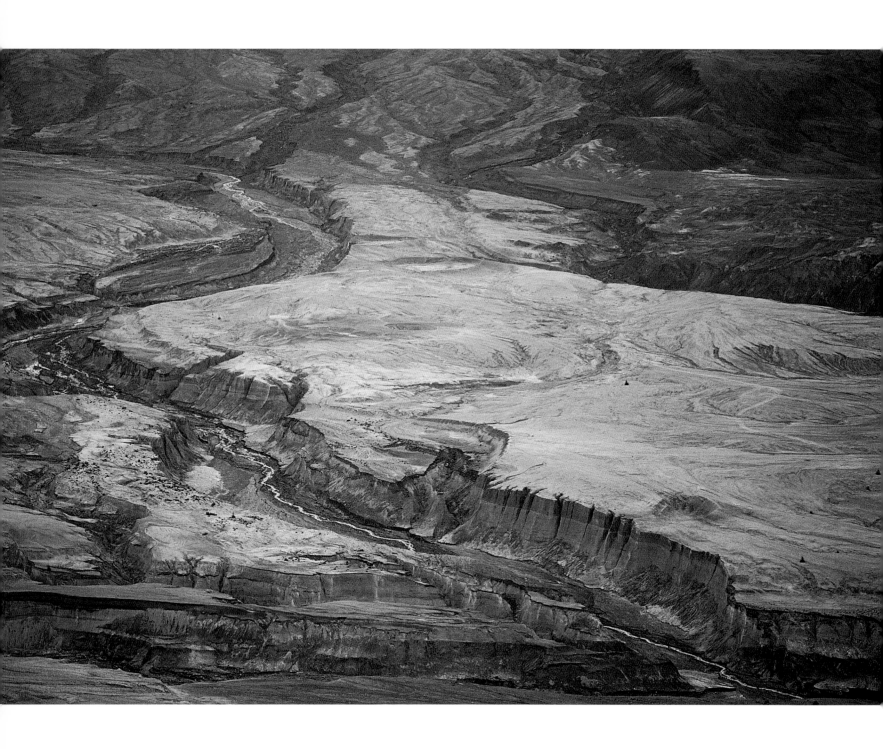

FOREWORD

At 8:30 A.M. on Sunday, May 18, 1980, my plane took off from the Portland Airport for Spokane, where I had been invited to give the commencement address at Whitworth College. At 8:32 A.M. the pilot announced that Mount St. Helens was erupting. We were at about five thousand feet and, as the pilot banked the plane, you might say I had a grandstand seat on the fifty-yard line to observe the eruption.

It was so unreal and spectacular that it might have been a scene in a B-grade movie. Not only was the mountain belching forth smoke and ashes, but there were lightening-like flashes in all directions. We did not tarry long, but continued to Spokane and, needless to say, the rest of the flight was marked by commentary and review of the experience by the entire cabin. I arrived at Whitworth in time for the 2:00 P.M. processional.

There was beautiful sunshine in Spokane as we proceeded across the campus into the fieldhouse. The fieldhouse was windowless except for a strip of windows near the domed ceiling. About half an hour into the program, the college president leaned over and said, "Perhaps we should rearrange the order of the ceremony in order to free you up to leave so you can catch your plane." As he spoke, he pointed to the windows, which at that moment were totally dark, as if night had fallen in the early afternoon. The president indicated that southwesterly winds had brought the ash across the state, thus blocking out the sun as if it were nighttime.

My chief of staff, Gerry Frank, was traveling with me and had already noted this and had slipped out to reserve a hotel room in case we could not get our flight out of Spokane for Seattle and our return to Washington, D.C.

At 8:32 A.M. the pilot announced that Mount St. Helens was erupting. We were at about five thousand feet and, as the pilot banked the plane, you might say I had a grandstand seat on the fifty-yard line to observe the eruption.

◄ *The upper Toutle River valley.*

There were times that the

highway was so covered with

ash that the driver had to

gauge the roadway between

fence posts rather than by the

highway striping.

Most of the commencement audience was not aware, at this time, of what was happening outside. I made a very abbreviated statement as my address to the graduates (commencement audiences always appreciate brevity), and we departed, heading for the hotel downtown in a blizzard of ash.

By this time it was announced on the radio that the Spokane airport had been closed, the highway had been closed, the railroad was closed, and no public transportation out of Spokane was available.

The next morning, Monday, Gerry went out canvassing the taxi drivers and found one who was willing to venture out onto the highway to Seattle. He armed himself with a number of air filters to change during the trip as the filter was continuously being clogged by ash. We had many stops along the three-hundred-mile route, not only to change filters, but to get gas at the few stations open, and to eat a candy bar once in a while. There were times that the highway was so covered with ash that the driver had to gauge the roadway between fence posts rather than by the highway striping.

At the Seattle airport, we were able to get the red-eye back to Washington, D.C. twenty-four hours late. Arriving at my Senate office in Washington in the early hours of Tuesday, my secretary informed me that the White House was attempting to reach me. They informed me that President Carter was going to fly out to see the devastation caused by the mountain's eruption and was inviting Senator Warren Magnuson, chairman of the Appropriations Committee, and me as ranking Republican member of the same committee, to accompany him.

My first reaction was that it cost me $495 in taxi fares to get out of that area and here I was being invited to go back one day later. But, not wanting to miss an opportunity to join the President on Air Force One, I accepted, and Senator Magnuson and I accompanied President Carter to Portland where we transferred to a helicopter to view the devastation.

The mountain was still smoking as we flew over the crater and the surrounding wood lot. Hundreds of thousands of trees had been flattened by the eruption, making it look like a giant clear cut of the entire Mount St. Helens area.

We were met by Governor Dixie Lee Ray and state officials, and were given a briefing by forest officials of the monumental damage, including the loss of Harry Truman—not the President, but the recluse who had made his life on the mountain.

When President Carter asked Governor Ray what he could do to be most helpful, she retorted, "Just send money—m-o-n-e-y." Later, at the meeting of the Appropriations Committee called to pass an emergency bill, one of the members asked Chairman Magnuson what figure he had in mind and he said, "Oh, I think a billion dollars is a nice round figure." And a billion dollars it was, without any supporting data. In time, a plan was put into effect and evolved which ultimately fell short of that total.

For me, the most amazing aftermath experience came approximately two years later when I was flying from Portland to Seattle. The flight took us over Mount St. Helens and here was this moonscape of total desolation that I had viewed back on May 21, 1980, just after the eruption. But now the marvelous color of green seedling Douglas-firs was poking through as the miraculous healing process of regeneration had already begun.

At about the same time, in August, 1982, President Reagan signed into law a bill establishing the Mount St. Helens National Volcanic Monument—an area immediately around the crater that would be left to evolve without replanting or other human intervention; a magnet for science and public visitation.

The places shown and stories revealed in this book's photographs, occurring both inside and outside the Volcanic Monument, are the legacy of the natural events I was fortunate to observe and the human responses in which I was privileged to participate.

—Mark O. Hatfield,
United States Senator (retired)

For me, the most amazing aftermath experience came approximately two years later. Now the marvelous color of green seedling Douglas firs was poking through as the miraculous healing process of regeneration had already begun.

► *The setting sun as seen from Windy Ridge.*

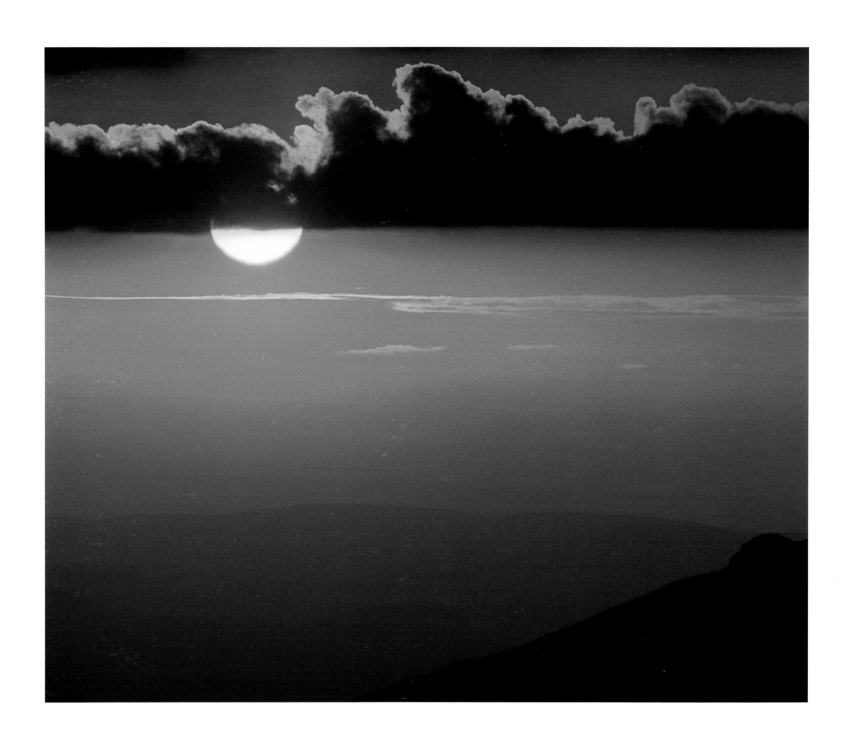

She dances,
she dances,
the lady dances.
Ashes, ashes, all fall down!
Shakti, Shakti,
blew your stack,
your virgin crown
is boiling mud,
forestfire, earthshake,
gas, ash, filth, flood,
your breath death. You are
a darkness on the western wind,
a curtain falling for a thousand miles.
O lady you've blown it,
you're grit between our teeth,
motes in our eyes,
rose-salmon sunsets clear to Reykjavik.
Your face is dirty, seamed, burnt, scarred.
You killed the old man and his cats,
ten billion tiny fish,
and broke the lake your mirror.
Bad luck lady.
The grey Quaker woke
and the cities of the plain
beheld, and shook,
cast ashes on their heads,
crying Lady be good!
Unkind: O plumed
unmaker,
fire-womb,
O dancer!   (4 June 1980)

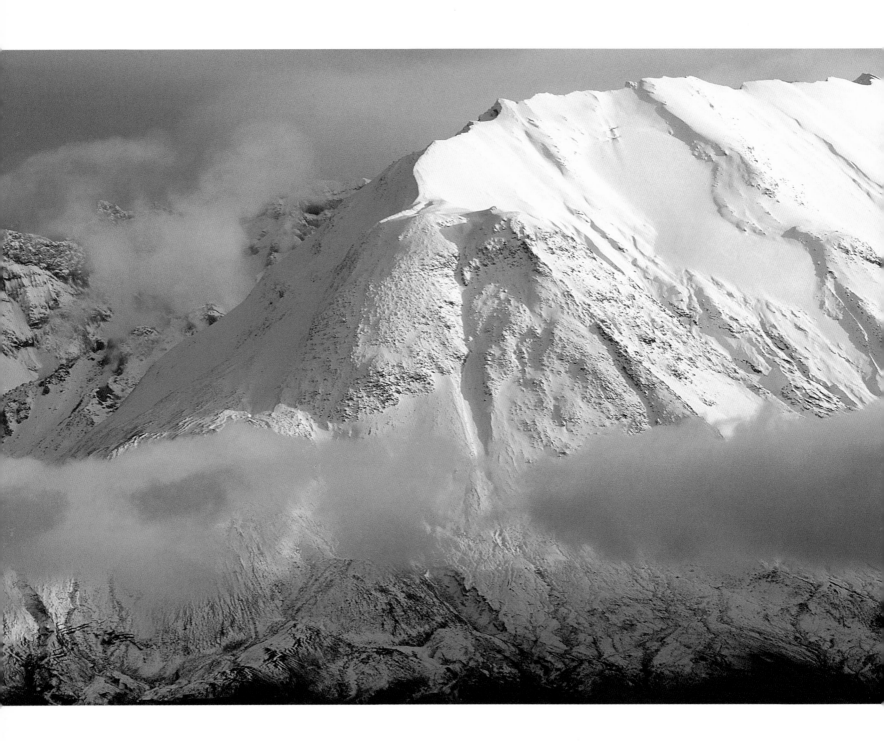

INTRODUCTION:
AN UNEXPECTED LANDSCAPE

On May 18, 1980, I was enjoying a quiet Sunday morning at home. When word of the eruption of Mount St. Helens reached me, I recall going to a high vantage point in my Seattle neighborhood to see if the ash plume was visible rising into the sky over a hundred miles away. But my thoughts soon turned to what tasks would await me the next day at the office. At the time I was director of raw materials R & D at Weyerhaeuser, which owned forestlands in the immediate vicinity of the mountain.

Not too long afterward, colleagues and I landed by helicopter in the midst of the destruction. It was as otherworldly a scene as I hope to experience. Not knowing if or when the next "volcanic event" might occur, the helicopter rotor stayed spinning, the pilot remained at the controls monitoring the emergency frequency on the radio, and our group never moved out of earshot. In every direction, it was the same lifeless gray: the collapsed mountain, the shattered tree remnants, the barren landscape, all covered with pumice and ash. We were there to gather data to help answer questions such as whether the remains of forests could be collected for paper and lumber? Could seedlings be planted and survive? (In the months that followed, my co-workers concluded that outside of the areas closest to the volcano, trees blown down by the blast from the mountain could be salvaged and remarkably, seedlings could indeed survive.) Technical issues related to Mount St. Helens occupied a good share of my workdays for quite a while.

In subsequent years, I drove the few U.S. Forest Service roads open to the public and flew over the area by helicopter several more times. During the

Not knowing if or when the next "volcanic event" might occur, the helicopter rotor stayed spinning, the pilot remained at the controls monitoring the emergency frequency on the radio, and our group never moved out of earshot.

◄ *The crater and west side of Mount St. Helens.*

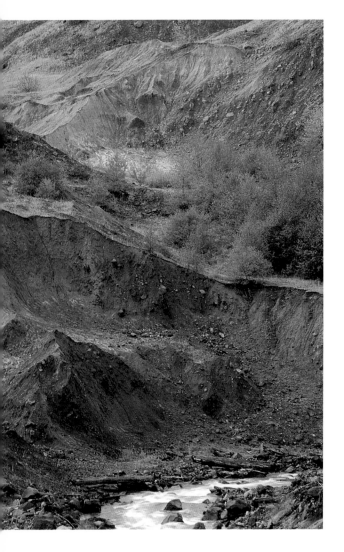

▲ *A creek cuts through landslide material*
from the mountain's north face.

1990's, and after my days with Weyerhaeuser, a resurrected State Highway 504 was built in the hills above its earlier route buried beneath volcanic debris in the Toutle River valley. My first time on that road brought back many memories. It was dawn and there was not another person anywhere to be seen. As I drove toward the mountain, I thought back to pre-1980 trips into the same area. I also recalled an early post-eruption visit with my Dad to what was then the end of the old road at the site of the Debris Dam put up by the Corp of Engineers soon after the blast. The dam failed in subsequent winters and the place he and I had stood is now under water and mud. At the time, we had also climbed to the top of a nearby hill for a better view. That hilltop is close to the rebuilt road and Hoffstadt Bluffs Visitor Center, and from there I could now peer down on the spot my Dad and I had been in the early 1980's, with nothing but a freshly rearranged landscape all around us.

The new highway ends at Johnston Ridge, directly north of Mount St. Helens. It was eerie to stand there again, looking directly into the crater of the volcano. I had last been on this ridge when our helicopter landed there some years after the eruption. It was then a stark, empty place not yet named for geologist David Johnston, who had been killed on the ridge on the morning when the mountain exploded. After all these years, whenever I am alone near the volcano, I find that I still keep a wary eye on the crater for signs of the next eruption.

Immediately after the eruption, most predictions were that it would be years before life returned, if at all. Yet, on my early visits I was amazed to see both pockets of vegetation and significant numbers of elk in the impact zones. Every time I go back—in all seasons and weather conditions—I am impressed by the contrasting patterns of recovery. Many areas continue to rapidly fill with plants and animals, yet other areas seem immune and look almost as they did on that first post-eruption helicopter trip. Mount St. Helens is always surprising.

A BIT OF HISTORY

Humans have inhabited the immediate vicinity around Mount St. Helens for more than ten thousand years. For Northwest native peoples, the foothills were a place to visit for hunting and berry gathering, but not to linger. Legends tell of fire, smoke, and rocks coming from the volcano. The first Europeans to see the mountain were members of George Vancouver's HMS Discovery expedition in 1792. They named it after British countryman Baron St. Helens.

Logging opportunities and mining exploration brought significant activity to the area at the end of the nineteenth century. A dirt road built along the North Fork of the Toutle River to support these commercial enterprises reached all the way to Spirit Lake at the northeast base of the mountain by 1901. While mining never developed, forestry became an important part of the story of Mount St. Helens. In about 1910, the public lands surrounding the mountain were included in what has become the present day Gifford Pinchot National Forest. At the start of 1980, the extensive timberlands on all sides of Mount St. Helens formed a checkerboard of private and public ownership and all were actively managed.

The early logging roads also opened the forests to recreational uses, with several youth camps established by 1913 on the shores of Spirit Lake. In 1938, about twenty-five thousand summer visitors came to the area. Most roads near the mountain remained unpaved until after World War II. By 1980, the foothills of Mount St. Helens hosted many popular public campgrounds, several seasonal resorts, and hundreds of get-away cabins and summer homes. All of this human presence was swept away in minutes when the dormant volcano awoke.

THE ERUPTION

Mount St. Helens' volcanic history goes back forty thousand years, with the

For Northwest native peoples, the foothills were a place to visit for hunting and berry gathering, but not to linger. Legends tell of fire, smoke, and rocks coming from the volcano.

Soon the north face of the

mountain began growing

rapidly, producing a large

unstable bulge as pressure

built from molten rock and

gases flowing upward beneath

the surface. The bulge grew

steadily by as much as five

to eight feet each day!

dome of the mountain building up and erupting away many times. It is the most active Cascade Mountains volcano, though it had been quiet since 1857.

Earthquakes and steam eruptions beginning in late March of 1980 signaled the start of another active period. Soon the north face of the mountain began growing rapidly, producing a large unstable bulge as pressure built from molten rock and gases flowing upward beneath the surface. The bulge grew steadily by as much as five to eight feet each day!

On the morning of May 18, triggered by an earthquake, the bulge gave way, unleashing an enormous landslide that sent much of the north side and summit of the mountain racing outward at one hundred miles per hour in a giant mass of rock, rapidly melted snow and ice. The landslide swept into the hills directly north of Mount St. Helens, and in some places even over-topped the thousand foot high Johnston Ridge. A portion of the landslide slammed into Spirit Lake, creating a two hundred foot wall of water that rushed away from the mountain and high up the sides of the valley at the far end of the lake. The landslide rebounded off the hills it encountered and then rolled down the North Fork of the Toutle River in a massive *debris avalanche* that now included parts of mountain, melted glaciers, and shattered forest stands. When the avalanche came to rest ten minutes later, the debris stretched fifteen miles down the river valley.

The bulge on the mountain's north side had served as a "lid" holding in the hot gases below the surface. As soon as the landslide removed this cover, the gases—accompanied by rocks from deep within the mountain—shot out the opening in a tremendous *lateral explosion*, moving at up to seven hundred miles per hour and with a temperature of six hundred degrees. This powerful, dark cloud traveled low to the ground, following the contours of the land up, over, and down the ridges and valleys. It ripped out and pulverized everything in its path, leaving behind a seared, empty landscape extending for five to seven miles over a fan-shaped area north of the erupting mountain. This area of complete devastation is now called the *inner blast zone*. Beyond five miles—and in places out to seventeen miles from the crater—the explosion's force knocked entire forests over, creating the huge *blowdown zone*. The dramatic long curves, formed by the trees left lying on the ground, revealed the pattern of flow of the passing gas and rock. The cloud eventually lost the force to topple trees, but it was still hot enough to scorch and kill them, producing a relatively narrow *standing dead zone* on the fringe of destruction. The lateral explosion covered over two hundred square miles in just minutes.

The heat of the eruption rapidly melted over seventy percent of the snow and ice on the summit's flanks, resulting in thick volcanic *mudflows*—also called *lahars*—descending on all sides of the mountain and into river channels. Especially impacted were the Muddy River, Smith Creek, Pine Creek and the South Fork of the Toutle River. The largest mudflow occurred on the North Fork of the Toutle, as the water captured inside the debris avalanche from melted snow, the upper reaches of the river, and even from Spirit Lake came gushing out, carrying huge amounts of dirt and rock with it downstream.

Shortly after the initial landslide, a one-thousand degree hot brew of pumice overflowed the crater and for several hours moved out of the volcano in a *pyroclastic flow* that formed a *pumice plain* at the northern base of the mountain. In the months and years that followed, this easily eroded material was shaped by water from rains and seasonal snowmelts into a landscape of vertical canyons and waterfalls beginning at the lower edge of the crater.

The landslide and the lateral explosion were followed by an ash plume venting for nine hours out of the ruptured mountain, quickly reaching an altitude of over sixty thousand feet and then drifting generally eastward.

In two weeks, traces of ash arrived back at Mount St. Helens after circling the globe.

The ash rising from the new crater was the image shown around the world at the time of the eruption. Ash caused numerous problems as it settled on vast

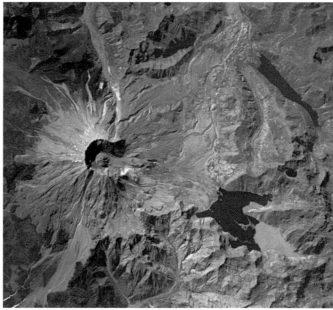

NASA Space Shuttle Photograph   (North is to the right.)

This powerful, dark cloud

traveled low to the ground,

following the contours of

the land up, over, and down

the ridges and valleys.

It ripped out and pulverized

everything in its path.

It was the landslide,

lateral explosion, and

mudslides that caused in

just minutes the dramatic

reshaping of the mountain

and that was most

responsible for creating

the startling landscapes

we see today.

areas and affected weather worldwide. Yet it was the landslide, lateral explosion, and mudslides that caused, in just minutes, the dramatic reshaping of the mountain and that was most responsible for creating the startling landscapes we see today. The landslide covered the pre-eruption ground with debris to a thickness averaging one hundred fifty feet, and up to five hundred feet in places. It deposited large, intact chunks of Mount St. Helens in the form of hummocks far from their previous locations high on the mountain. Material added to Spirit Lake raised its surface almost two hundred feet in elevation. The mudflow on the North Fork of the Toutle River carried material seventy miles to the Columbia River, destroying roads, bridges, and two hundred homes in its path. Thousands of animals died. Fifty-seven people were killed. Numerous accounts of frightening escapes emerged in the days that followed. The human toll would have been even greater if not for the facts that the eruption was on a Sunday when commercial logging operations were suspended and that the State of Washington had declared a no-entry zone immediately around the volcano.

Several smaller eruptions followed in 1980, and soon a new lava dome began building inside the crater—the start of a new summit.

Much more of the story of the eruption and its aftermath will be found in the photographs and captions in the pages that follow.

ABOUT THIS BOOK

Many fine books have been produced describing the 1980 eruption and the subsequent changes at Mount St. Helens. Here we have sought to convey the spirit of the place through photographs. The goal is to provide the feel of the area to the reader who has not yet visited the mountain and to provide evocative reminders for those who have ventured there. I am always startled by the sights that are displayed around each turn, and have tried to capture that sense of surprise and wonder in this book.

The photographs are arranged in four main chapters. The first chapter follows the main approach to the mountain from the west—up the North Fork of the Toutle River as far as Coldwater Lake. The next chapter covers the north side of the area, continuing from Coldwater Lake, up Johnston Ridge, and on to the crater. The images in the third chapter are all east of the mountain, moving from the volcano, past Spirit Lake, to the edge of the impact from the eruption. The final chapter visits the southern side of Mount St. Helens. Places mentioned in the captions can be found on the map on the following pages. A list of sources for further information is included at the back of the book.

Scattered throughout this book are sets of images from similar locations taken a decade or more apart. Some display surprising degrees of transformation. Other images reveal little apparent change since May 18, 1980. Mount St. Helens is a place of sameness and grayness co-existing with dramatic growth and color. For me, it is always a landscape of unexpected images.

—Mark Lembersky

Here we have sought to convey the spirit of the place through photographs. The goal is to provide the feel of the area to the reader who has not yet visited the mountain and to provide evocative reminders for those who have ventured there.

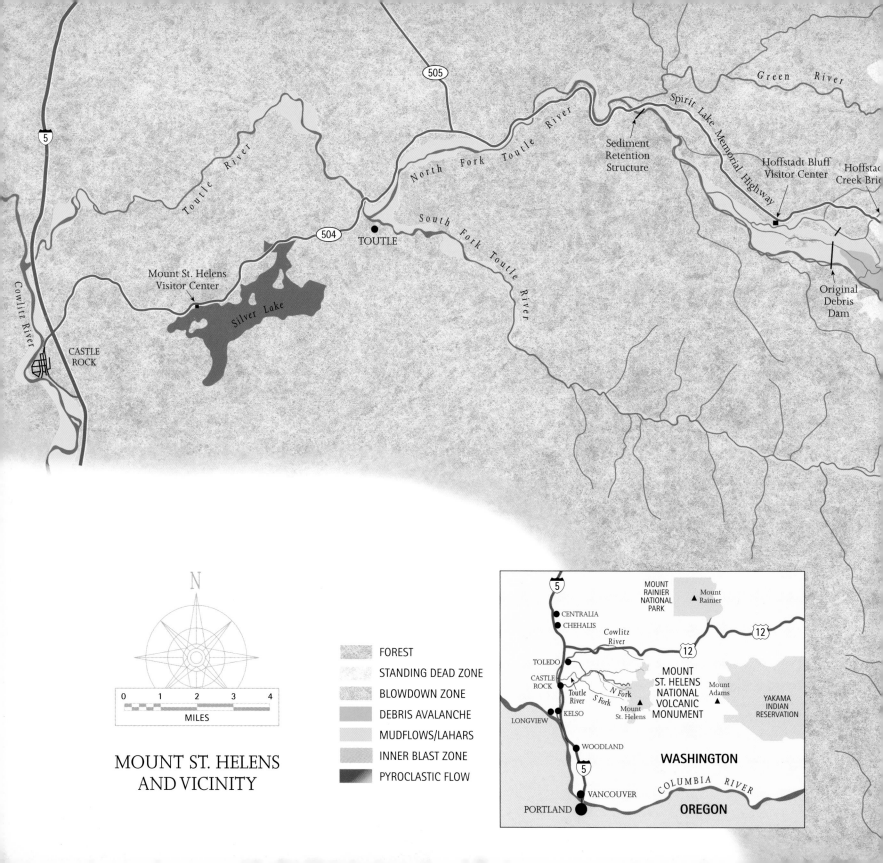

505

I-5

Toutle River

North Fork Toutle River

Green River

Spirit Lake Memorial Highway

Sediment Retention Structure

Hoffstadt Bluff Visitor Center

Hoffstad Creek Brid

504

TOUTLE

South Fork Toutle River

Mount St. Helens Visitor Center

Silver Lake

Original Debris Dam

Cowlitz River

CASTLE ROCK

N

0 1 2 3 4
MILES

MOUNT ST. HELENS
AND VICINITY

FOREST

STANDING DEAD ZONE

BLOWDOWN ZONE

DEBRIS AVALANCHE

MUDFLOWS/LAHARS

INNER BLAST ZONE

PYROCLASTIC FLOW

MOUNT RAINIER NATIONAL PARK

Mount Rainier

5

CENTRALIA

CHEHALIS

Cowlitz River

12

12

12

TOLEDO

CASTLE ROCK

Toutle River

N Fork

S Fork

MOUNT ST. HELENS NATIONAL VOLCANIC MONUMENT

Mount Adams

YAKAMA INDIAN RESERVATION

LONGVIEW

KELSO

Mount St. Helens

WOODLAND

5

WASHINGTON

VANCOUVER

COLUMBIA RIVER

PORTLAND

OREGON

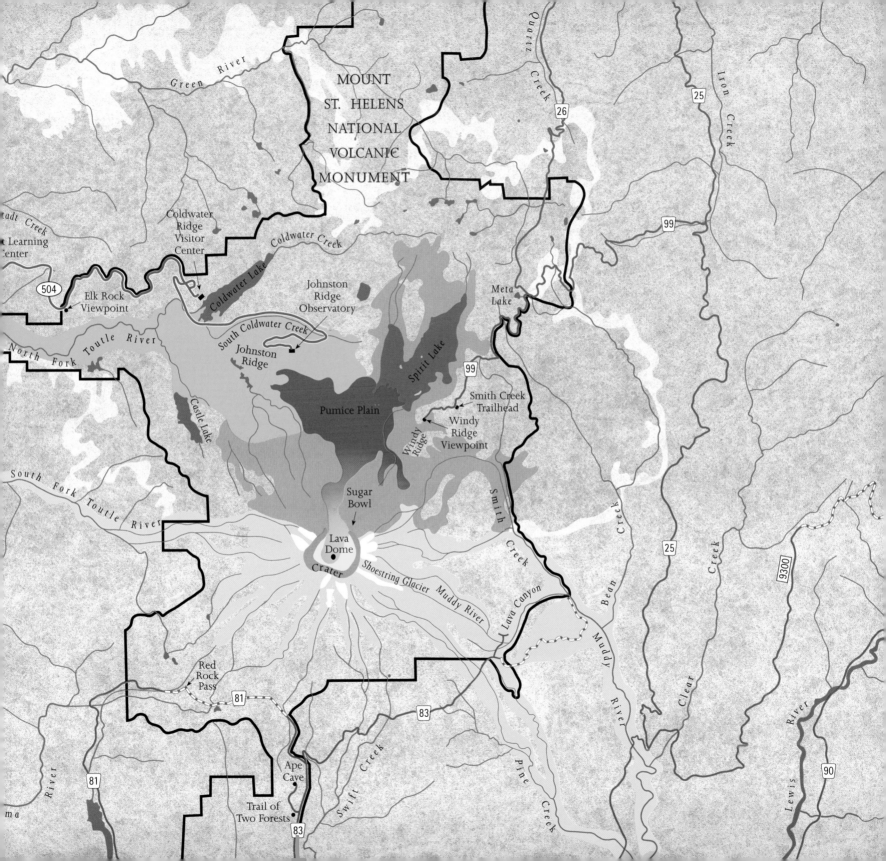

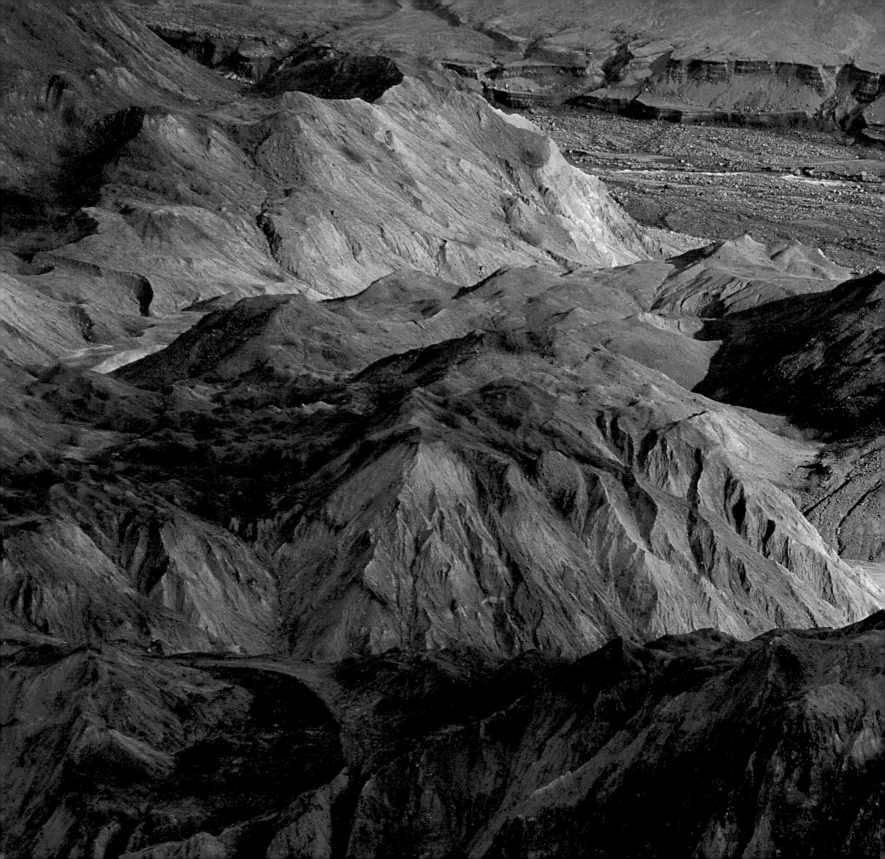

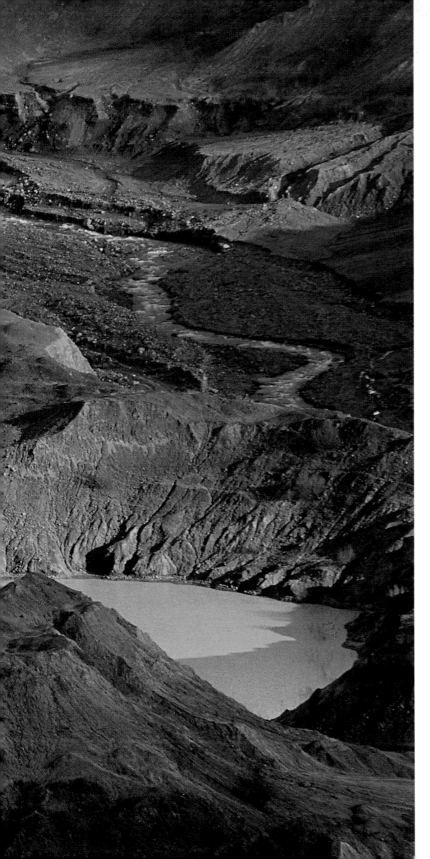

WEST
ALONG THE TOUTLE RIVER VALLEY

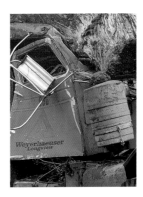

The western approach to Mount St. Helens is dominated by the effects of the debris avalanche and mudflow that went down the North Fork of the Toutle River. To a large extent, the massive amount of rock and earth that departed the mountain when it collapsed on May 18, 1980, is now in this river valley. Also evident today on the west side are vast areas that have been reclaimed, replanted, and boast new forests.

◄ *Former summit material deposited as hummock mounds by the debris avalanche. Beyond, the upper North Fork of the Toutle River winds through the volcanic residues.*

▲ *No forestry activity on the Sunday of the eruption saved many lives, but not this logging fire truck.*

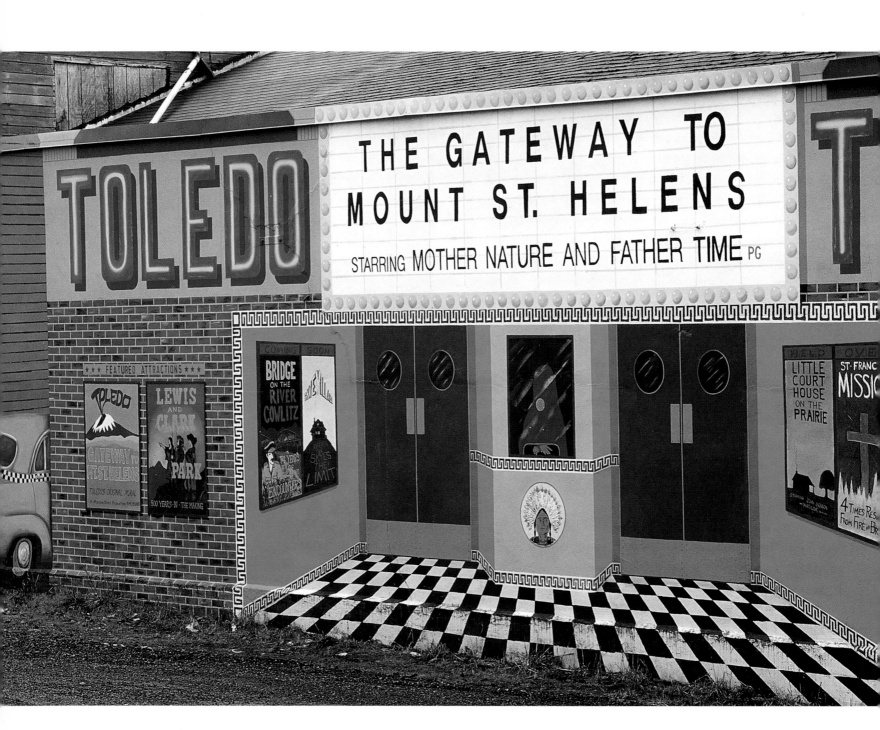

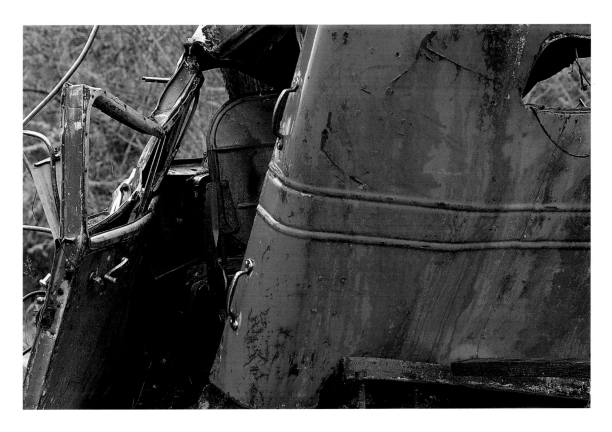

◄ *A wall mural along route 505 advertises the town of Toledo's claim to fame.*
▲ *and* ► *Vehicles caught in harm's way now displayed roadside near milepost 19 on route 504.*

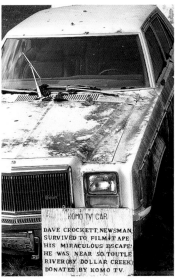

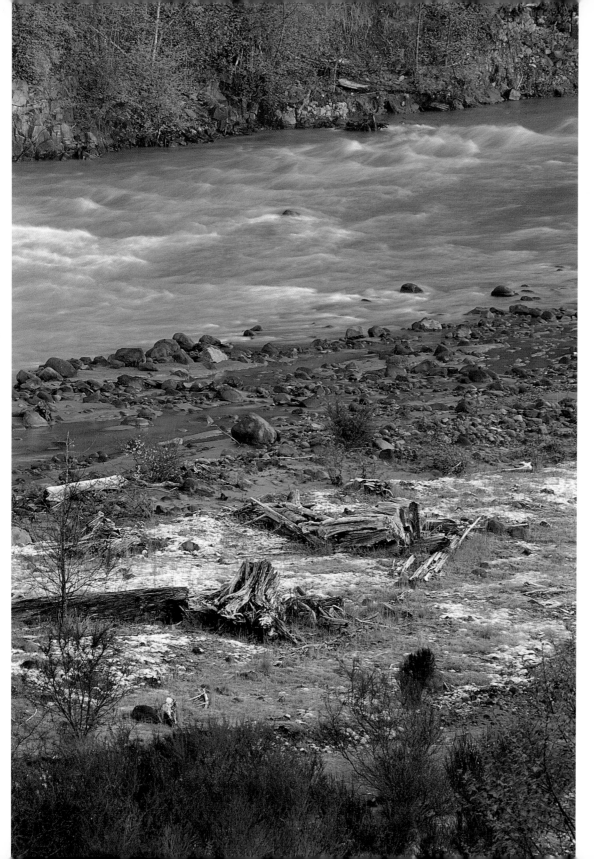

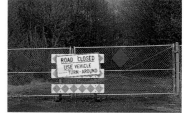

After the eruption, massive flooding was feared if large amounts of the debris in the North Fork of the Toutle River washed downstream with the winter rains and spring snowmelts, clogged rivers and waterways, and left no room for later water flows. To address this risk, the Army Corps of Engineers quickly built the Debris Dam near the foot of the avalanche deposits. When that dam failed, a more stout Sediment Retention Structure of earth and concrete was erected seven miles further downstream.

◄ North Fork of the Toutle River, a little west of the Sediment Retention Structure. This dam keeps most solids out of the river here and little indication remains of the thick mudflow that churned through in May of 1980.

◄ Beyond this sign at the Sediment Retention Structure, old route 504 continued east to Mount St. Helens and on to Spirit Lake. The road now lies buried under volcanic debris, part of the one hundred eighty-five miles of highways destroyed as a result of the eruption. The replacement route 504 is named the Spirit Lake Memorial Highway, but does not reach the lake.

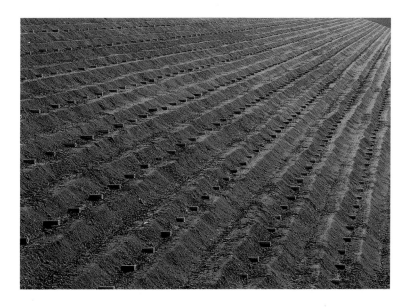

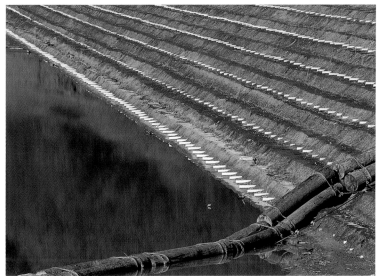

▲ and ◄ As the river meets the Sediment Retention Structure, seen here from both ends, sediments settle out and water drains through the pipes. As deposits rise, rows of pipes are sealed. When completed in 1989, the structure had one hundred twenty-five feet of height to accommodate sediments. Predictions are that the dam will fill with deposits by about 2035, when, it is hoped, clear water will spill over the top.

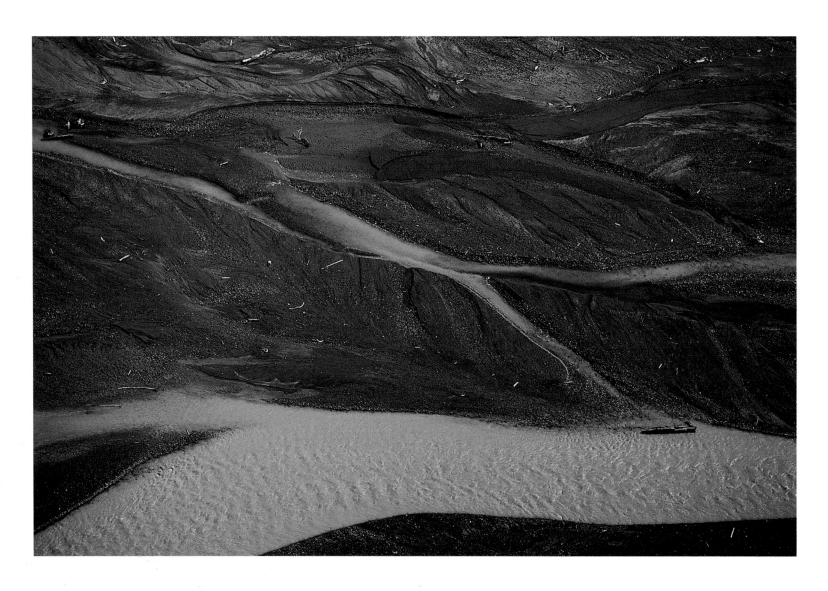

▲ The North Fork of the Toutle River above the Sediment Retention Structure. Compare with the view below the dam seen two pages earlier. Sediment movements on the river each of the first five years after the eruption were five thousand times pre-1980 levels.

► Logs swept up in the avalanche are exposed by the erosive action of the river on the volcanic debris.

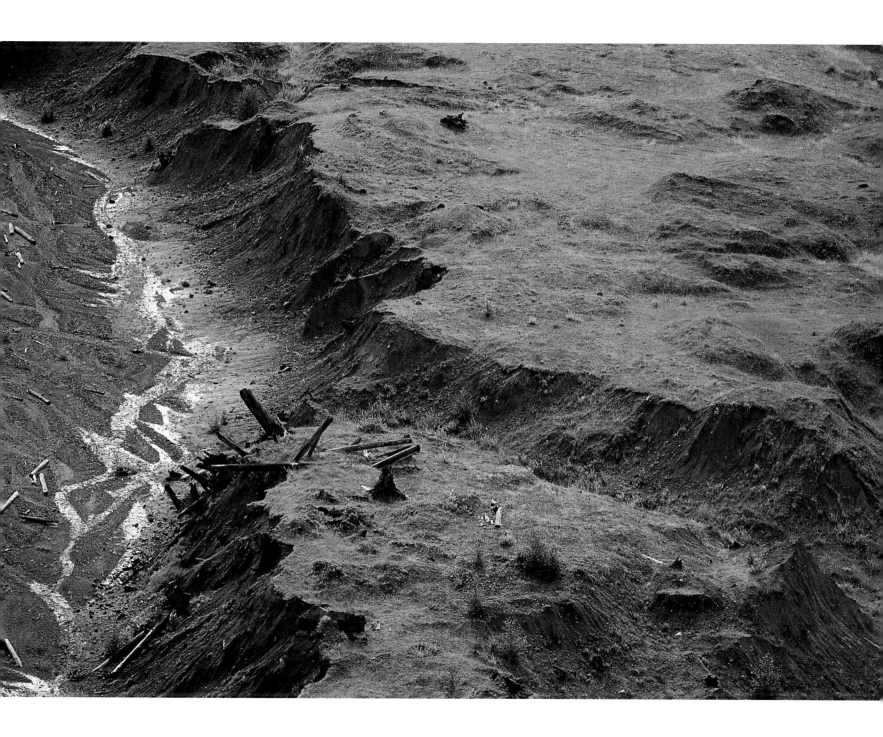

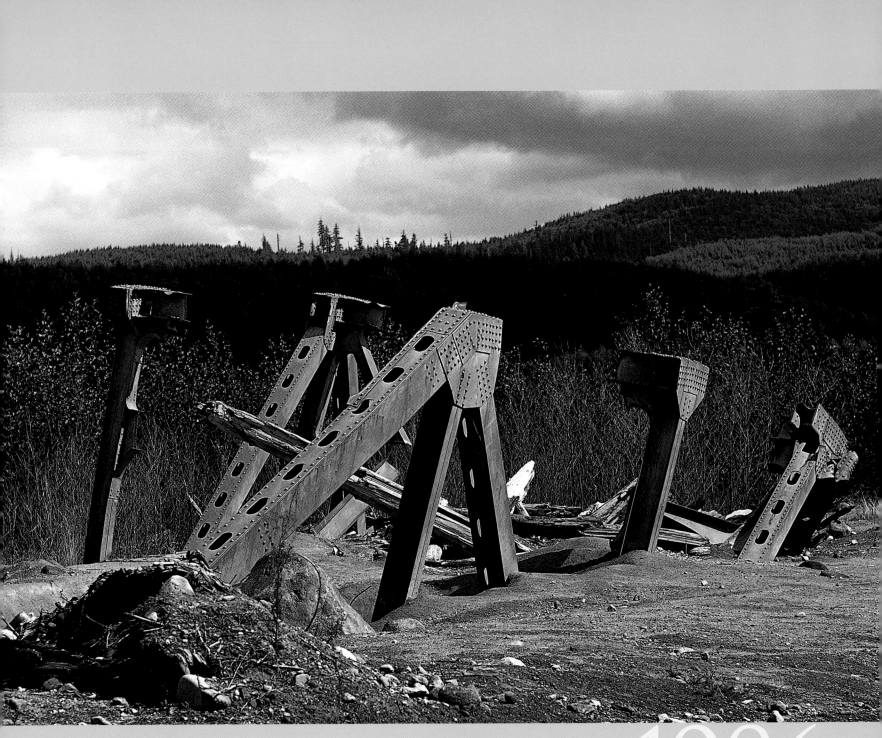

1986

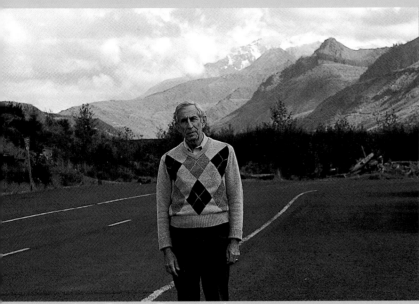

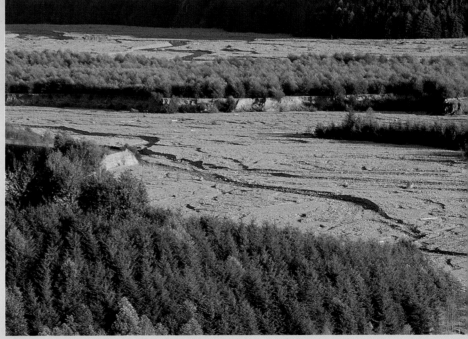

1999

1986

◄ One of the more than two dozen bridges damaged by mudflows. New route 504 was later built in the hills seen in the background.

▲ The end of the temporary road in 1986. Not far behind the visitor is the original forty foot high, more than mile wide Debris Dam built in the summer of 1980. Mount St. Helens is fifteen miles in the distance. The area in both 1986 photos became inundated in the years after the dam failed.

► The view from route 504, now high above the original Debris Dam site and former road end. Remaining dam segments can be seen at left-center and at the right edge.

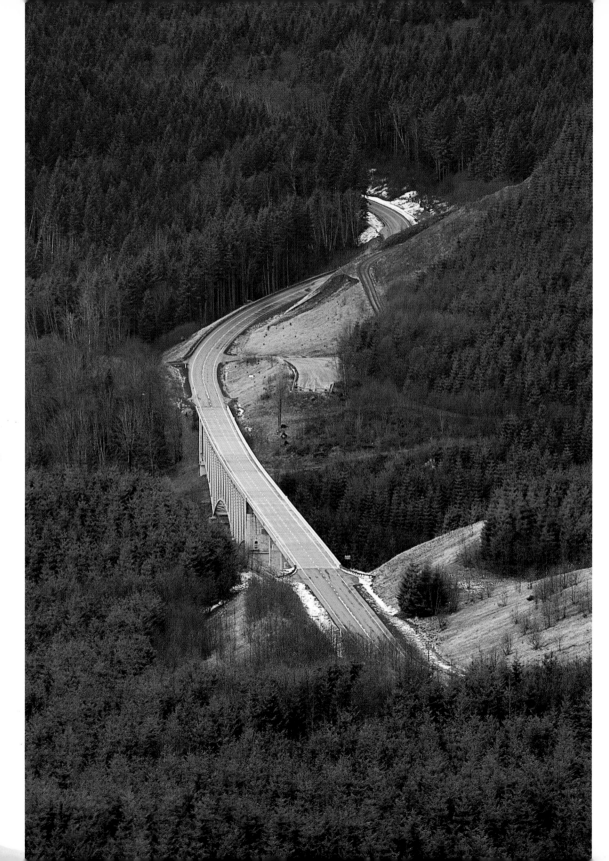

Large quantities of the blown down and standing dead trees outside the boundaries of the Mount St. Helens National Volcanic Monument were collected over a two year period beginning as soon as September of 1980. At its peak, this operation produced six hundred truckloads of logs a day. The salvage was followed in short order by tree planting.

▶ The western edge of the eruption's impact at half-mile long Hoffstadt Creek Bridge near route 504, milepost 30. At lower elevations such as this, primarily Douglas-fir seedlings were planted. Today in many such locations it is hard to detect evidence of the destruction.

▶▶ At a higher elevation and closer to the mountain, forest landowner Weyerhaeuser planted these noble fir. In the ten years after the eruption, Weyerhaeuser planted eighteen million seedlings on its lands near the volcano.

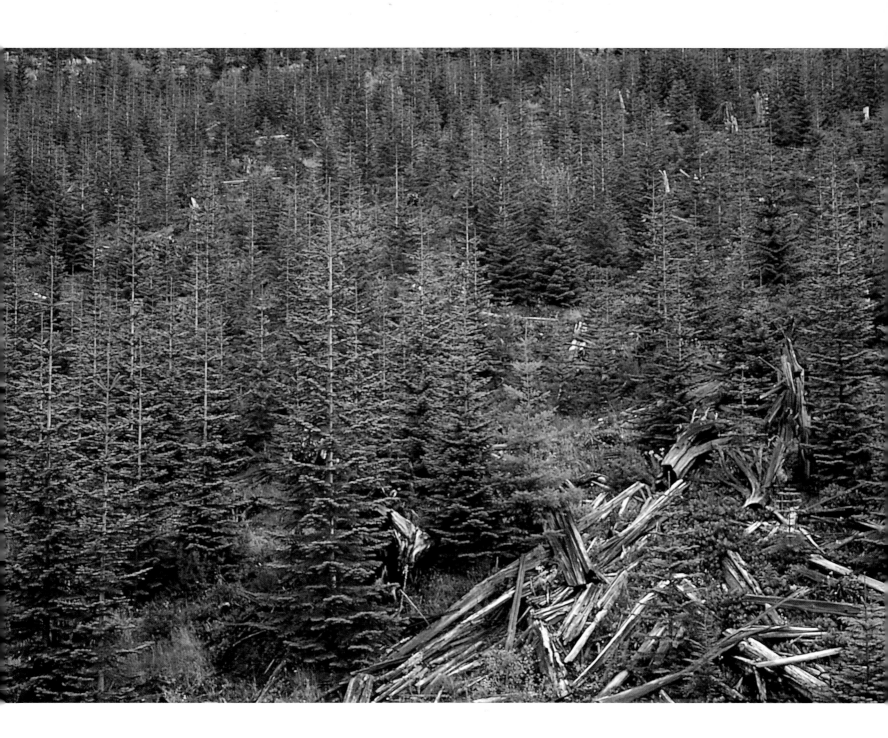

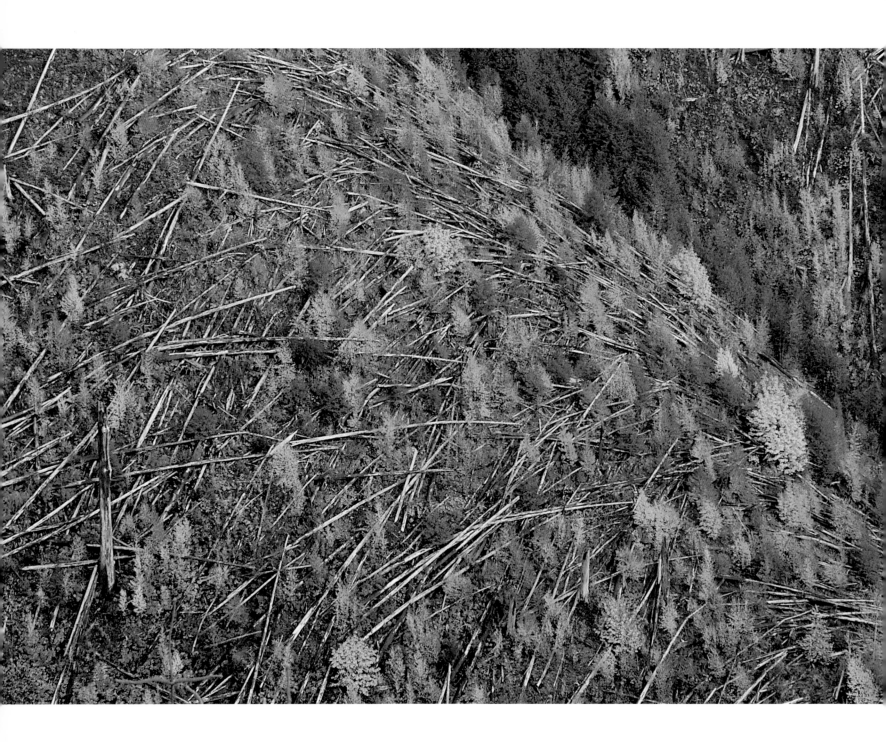

◄ In the blowdown zone within the Mount St. Helens National Volcanic Monument, trees have been left where they fell. Patterns in the downed trees reveal the path of the powerful lateral explosion that pushed them over. The blast damaged or destroyed well over three hundred million cubic feet of timber worth almost five hundred million dollars.

► and ▼ Seasonal changes in the blowdown zone.

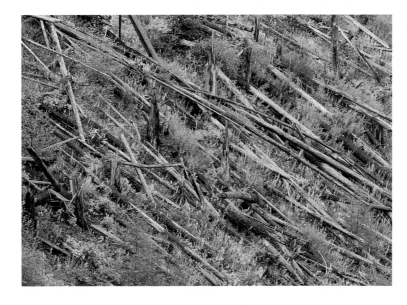

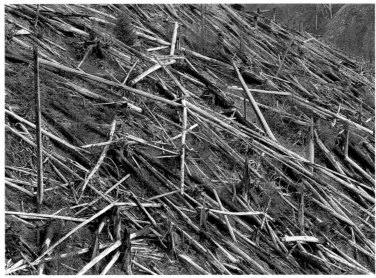

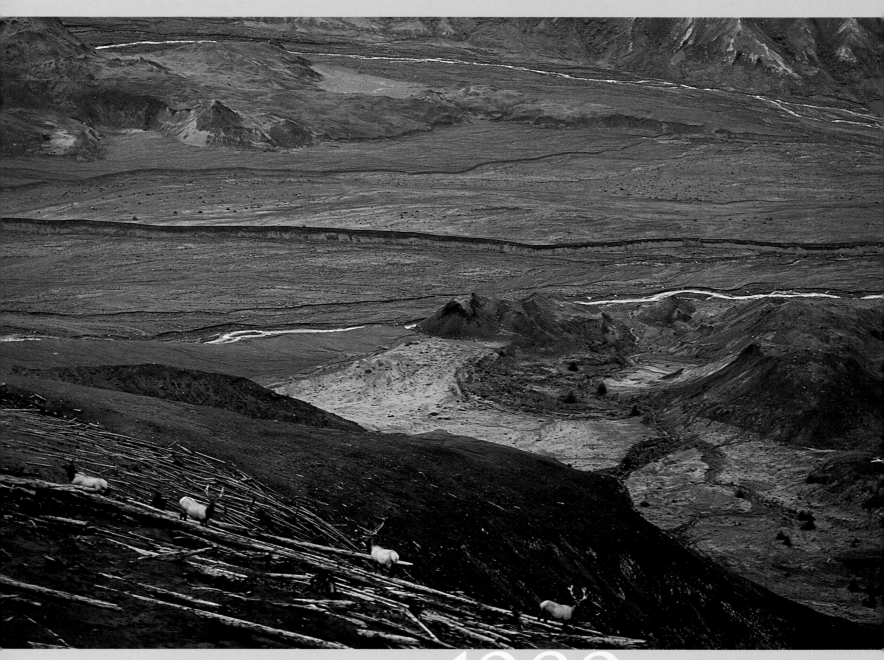

1989

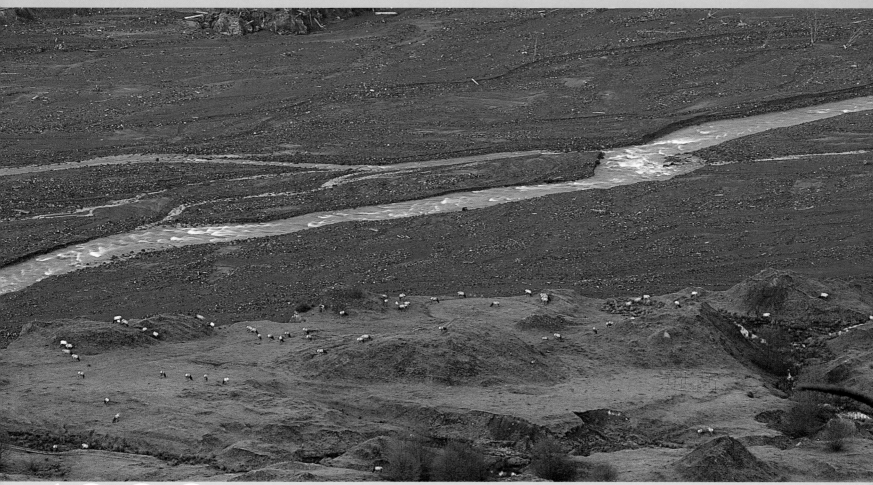

1999

The eruption killed five thousand deer and fifteen hundred elk in the impact zones. But large mammals soon returned.

◄ Elk were seen on the debris avalanche just weeks after the eruption. At the end of 1989, three times as many elk called Mount St. Helens home as before May, 1980.

▲ The number of elk continued to grow in the 1990's. As elk graze, their hooves mix buried soil and ash, making the ground more hospitable for green plants.

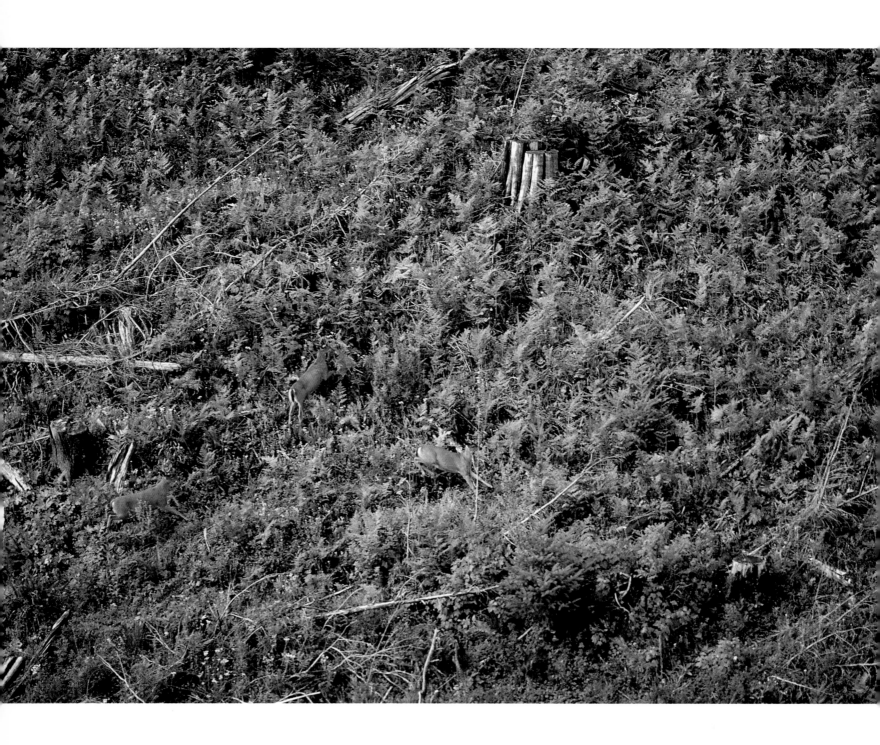

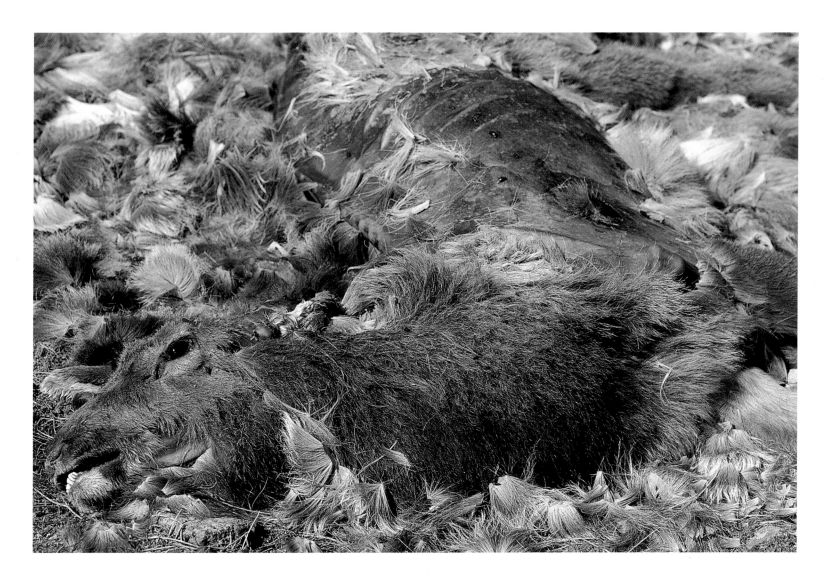

▲ Now, so many elk are present that a hard winter results in
many deaths, such as this victim of the winter of 1998-99,
when one-fifth of the herd starved.

◄ Deer frolicking ten years after the eruption.

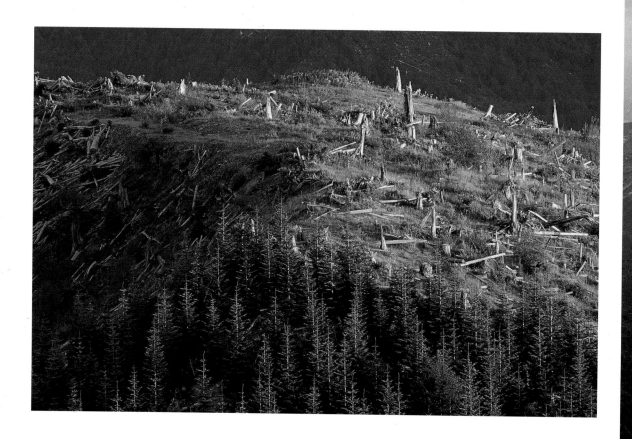

▲ *An exposed hilltop above the Toutle River valley at the edge of the Volcanic Monument still shows its scars from the impact of the lateral explosion twenty years earlier.*

▶ *Twilight view from Elk Rock up the Toutle River, with Johnston Ridge at the left and the pumice plain at the base of the volcano. Mount Adams is just visible above Johnston Ridge.*

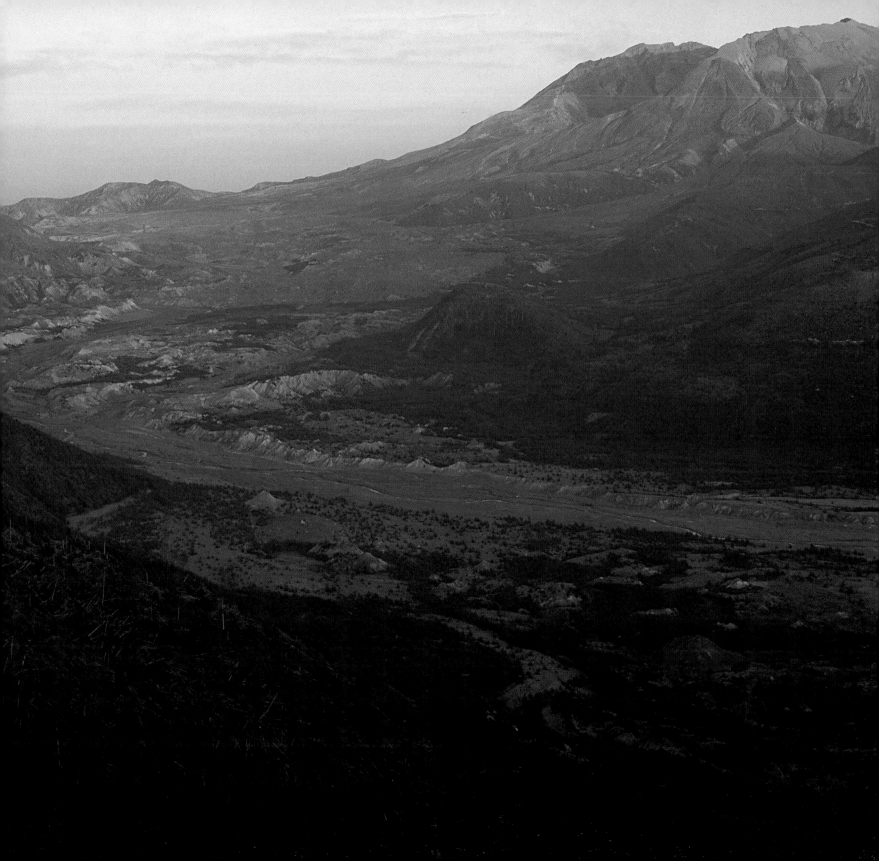

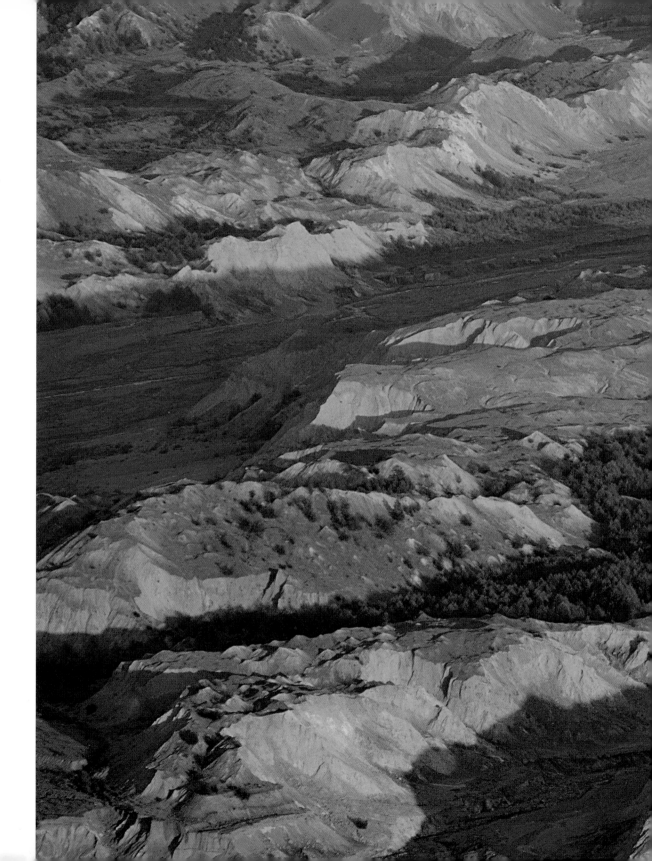

► Part of the debris avalanche that spread eighty billion cubic feet of material along the upper fifteen miles of the North Fork of the Toutle River.

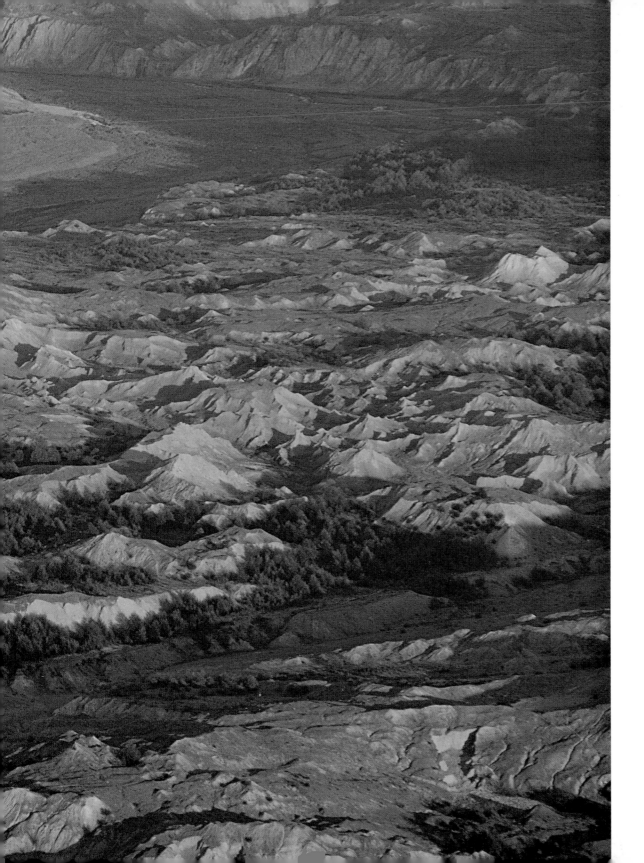

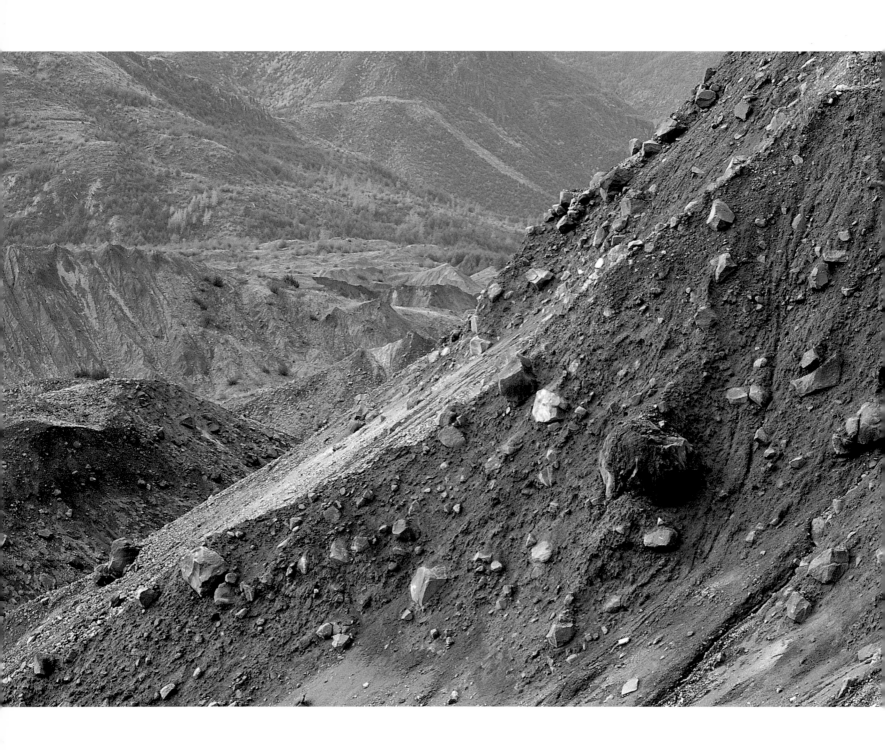

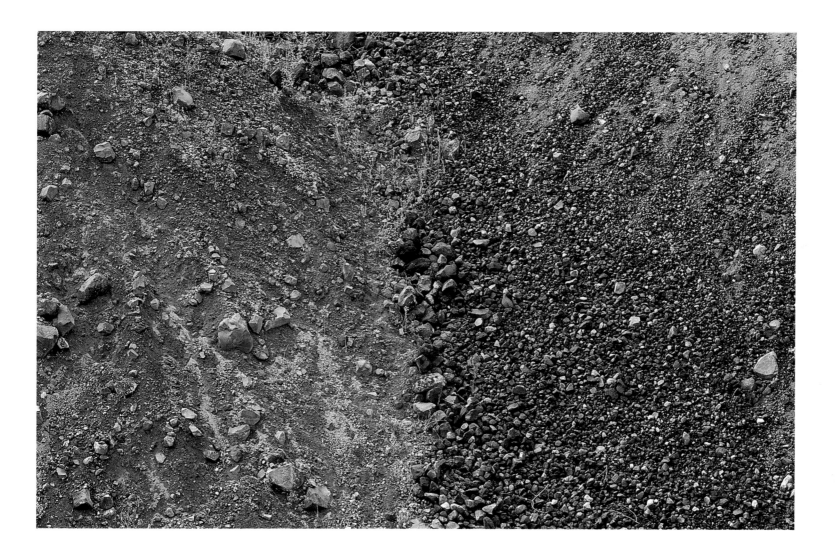

◄ Hummock mounds deposited just south of Coldwater Lake.

▲ These hummocks contain a mixture of various old and new volcanic materials.

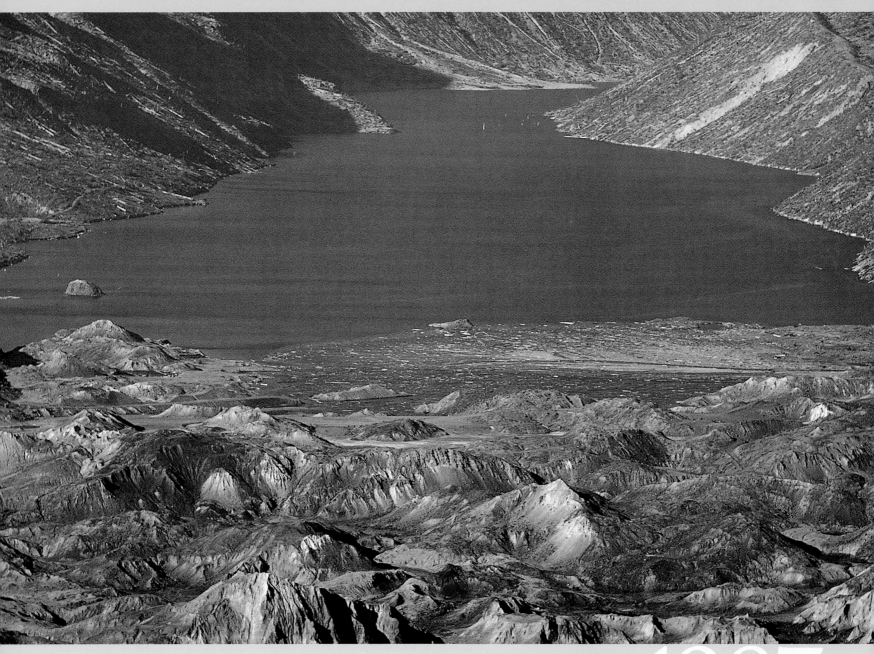

1987

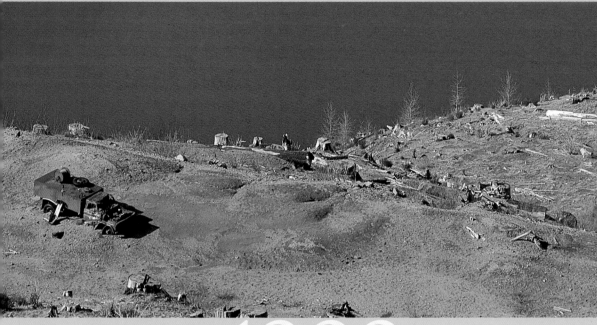

1999

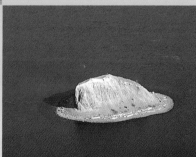

1999

◄ Coldwater Lake, which was formed when the debris avalanche deposits seen in the foreground blocked Coldwater Creek.

▲ A logging support truck remains in the spot where it was destroyed on the east side of what became Coldwater Lake. This area has changed little in twenty years.

► "Hummock Island," a large piece of Mount St. Helens blown to its current resting place in the midst of Coldwater Lake. It is also visible at the left in the 1987 photograph.

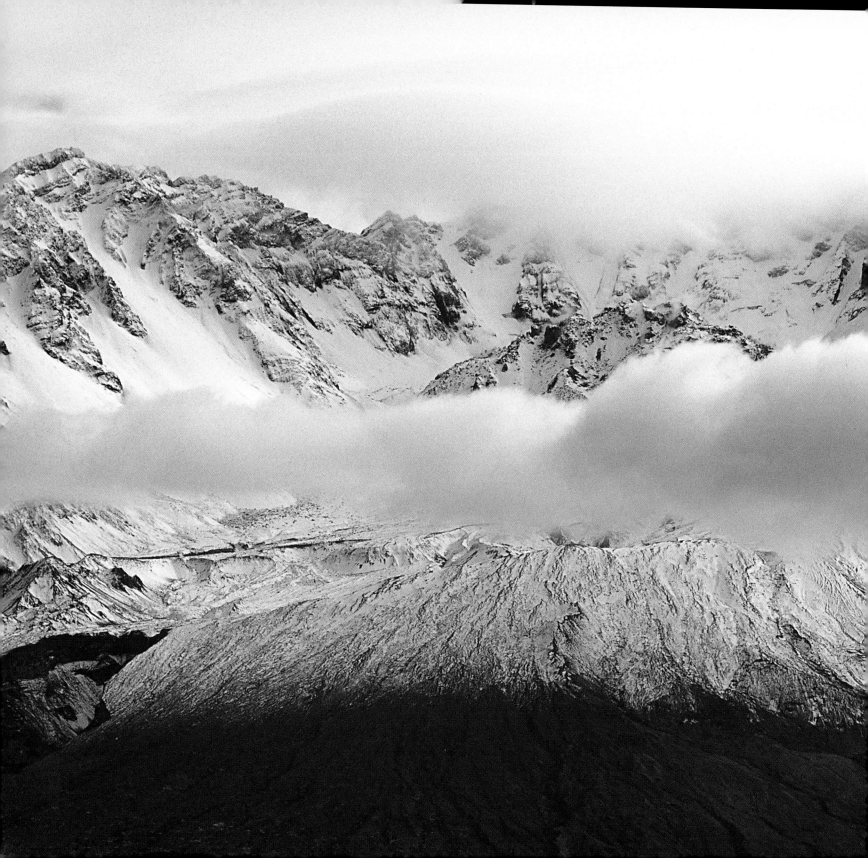

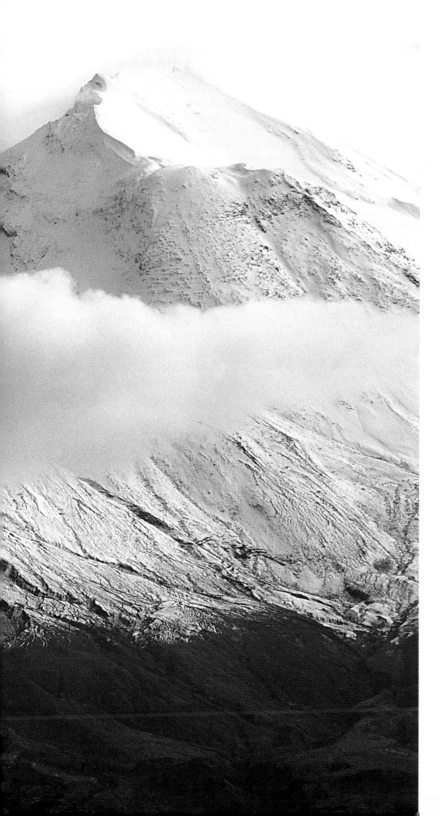

NORTH
ON TO THE CRATER

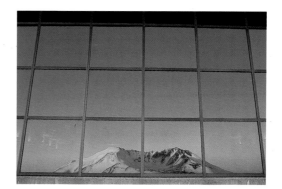

The area north, from Coldwater Lake to the volcano's crater, is the heart of the inner blast zone. There are pockets of revegetation, but this is the part of Mount St. Helens least changed since the 1980 eruption. Road access ends at the top of Johnston Ridge.

◄ *The eruption removed the summit, itself less than twenty-five hundred years old, reduced the mountain's height by thirteen hundred feet, and produced a crater two thousand feet deep and a mile and one-half wide.*

▲ *The volcano is reflected in the windows of the Johnston Ridge Observatory opened in 1997 and named, along with the ridge, for volcanologist David A. Johnston who died at his monitoring post when the eruption occurred.*

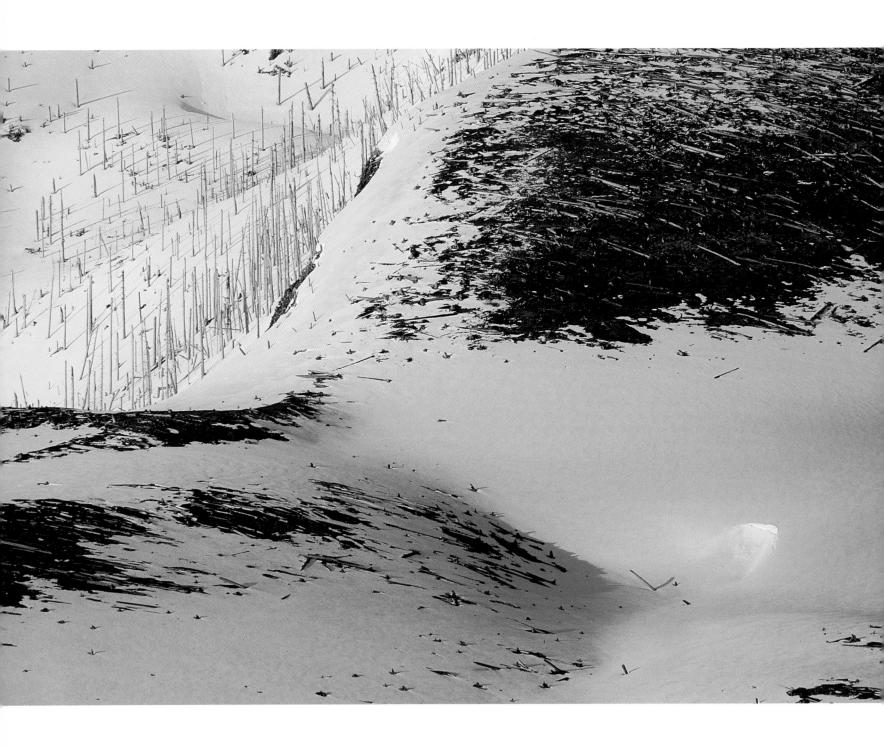

◄ On a peak seven miles north of the mountain, standing dead trees remain that were apparently sheared by the fast moving lateral explosion cloud as it came off the higher ground at right. There is no new vegetation in evidence at this high elevation area.

▼ Tree remnants along the bank of South Coldwater Creek in 1998.

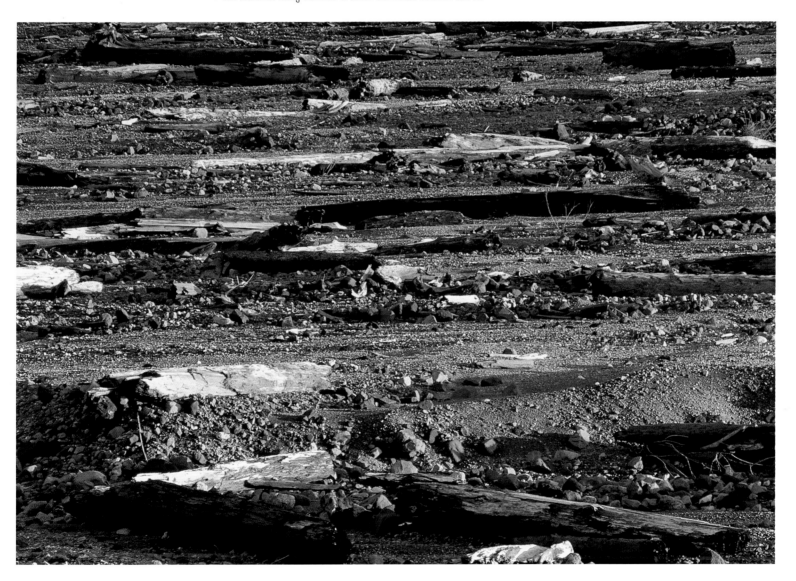

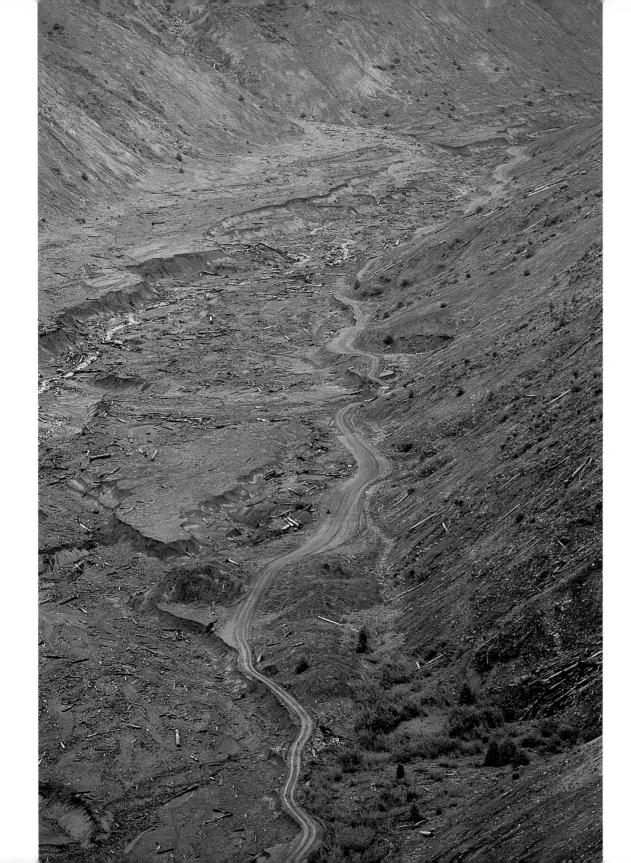

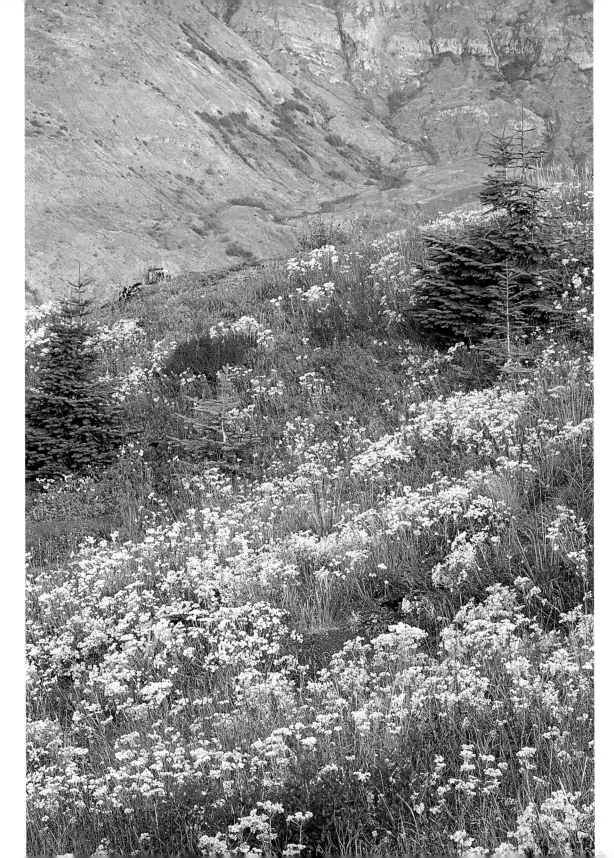

The landslide off the north face of the volcano at 8:32 A.M. on May 18, 1980 was so massive that in places it climbed over Johnston Ridge and spilled into the South Coldwater Creek basin located on the far side of the ridge.

◄◄ South Coldwater Creek in 1989, with Johnston Ridge at the right. A temporary road is seen on the right side of the creek; today route 504 runs on the opposite bank before crossing the creek to ascend the ridge.

◄ From the top of Johnston Ridge, looking north across South Coldwater Creek below. The foreground area was partially sheltered by the ridge and has vegetation in 1998, but the hillside across the creek took a powerful blast from the volcano and shows much less change.

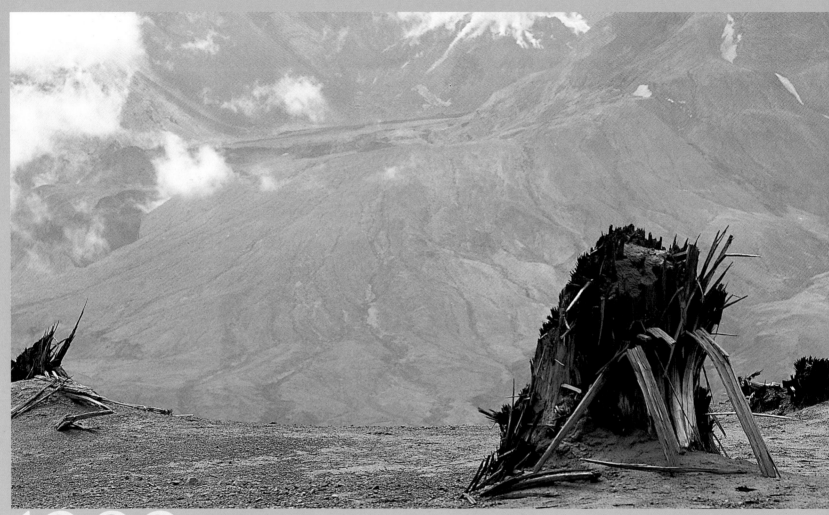

1989

▲ Johnston Ridge, lying so close to the volcano, received the direct impact of the lateral explosion that rocketed northward with tremendous force.

▶ Remarkably, what was dead and silent throughout the 1980's has become a popular destination at the end of the Spirit Lake Memorial Highway, approximately fifty miles east of the I-5 freeway. Visitors can peer straight into the crater from the Observatory now there.

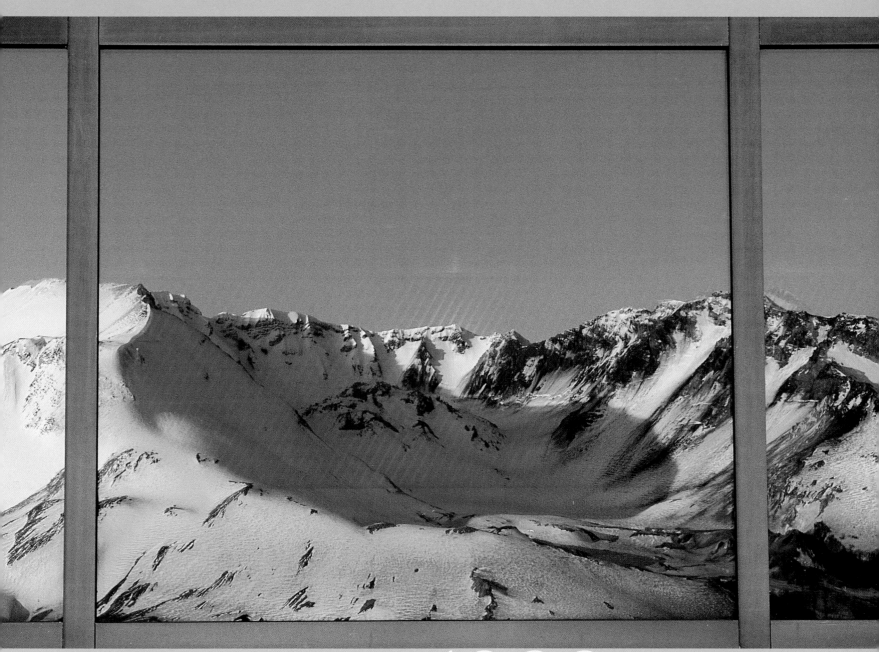

1999

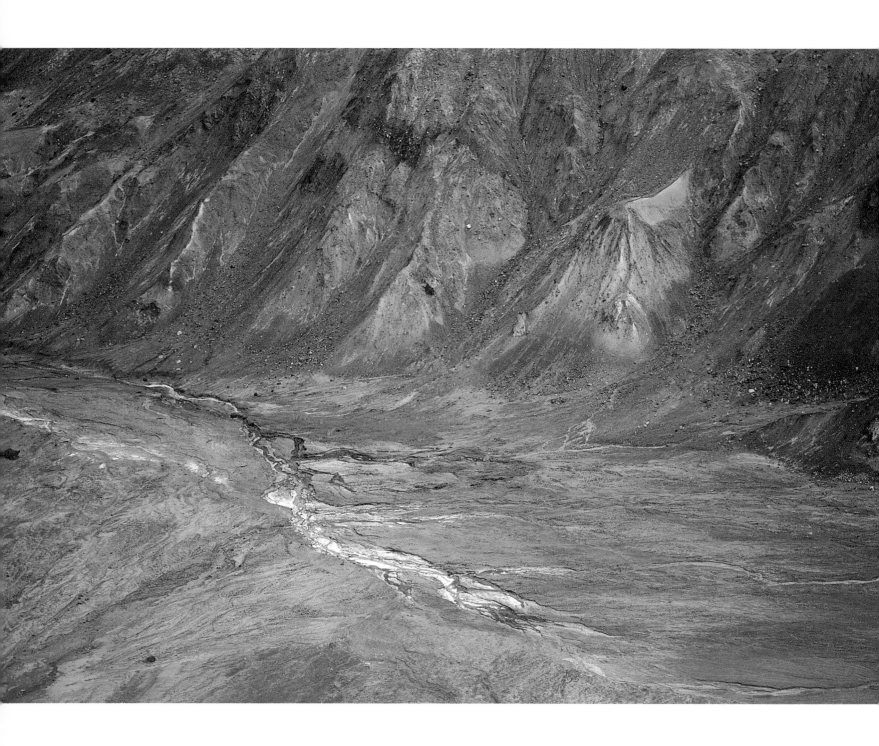

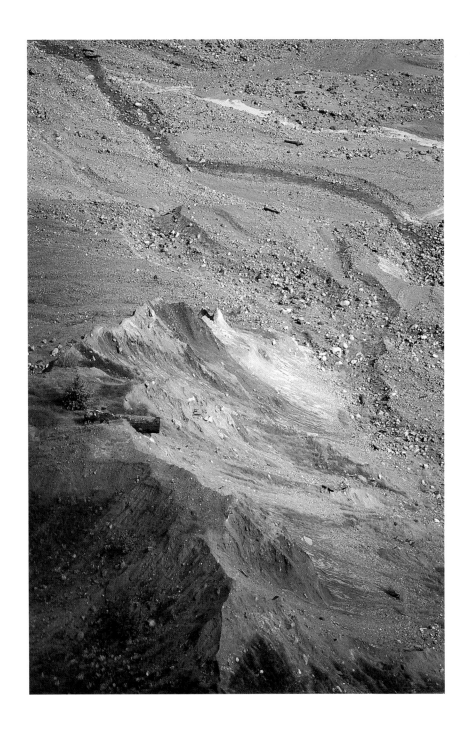

◄ and ► Two views of the
primal-looking landscape between
Johnston Ridge and the crater.

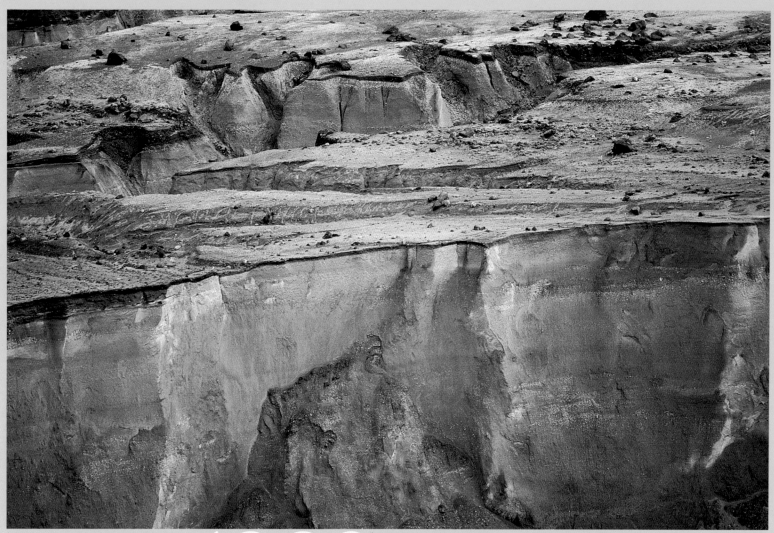

1989

▲ Immediately after the eruption, the pumice plain and uppermost debris avalanche areas were largely featureless, but rapid erosion produced steep-walled canyons.

▶ After an additional decade of weathering, the features are more rounded and some vegetation has appeared.

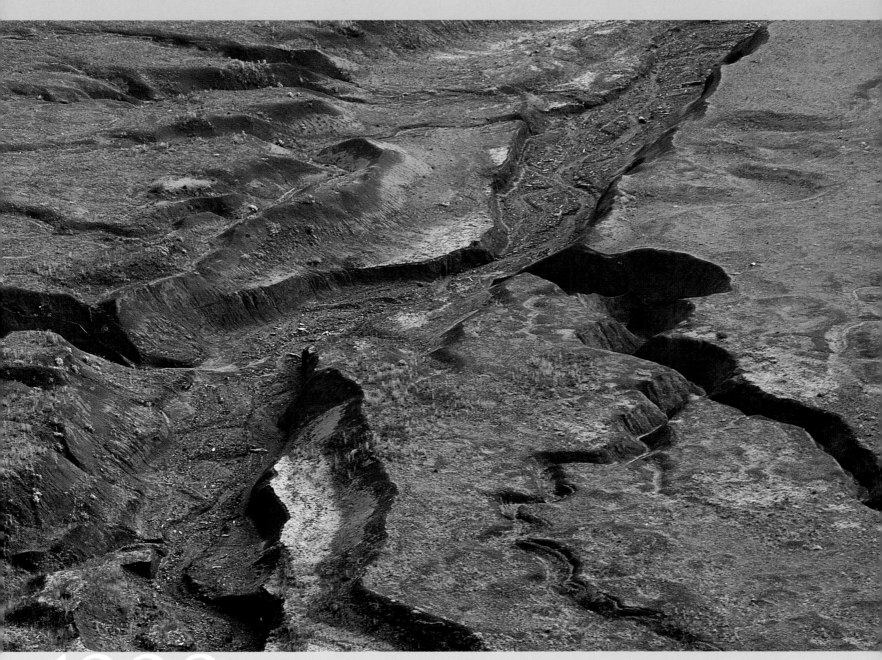

1998

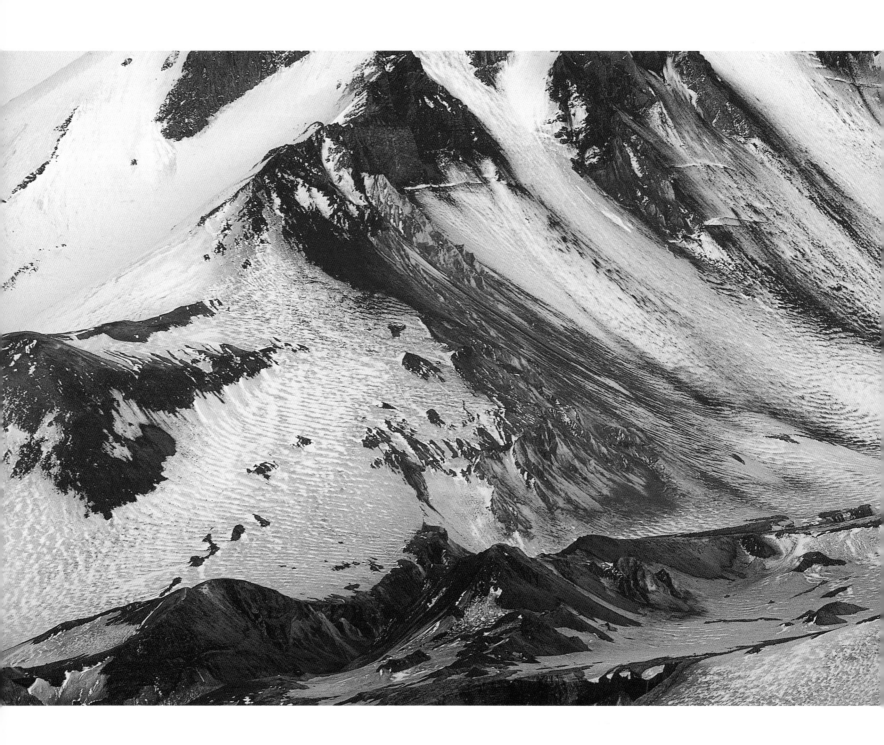

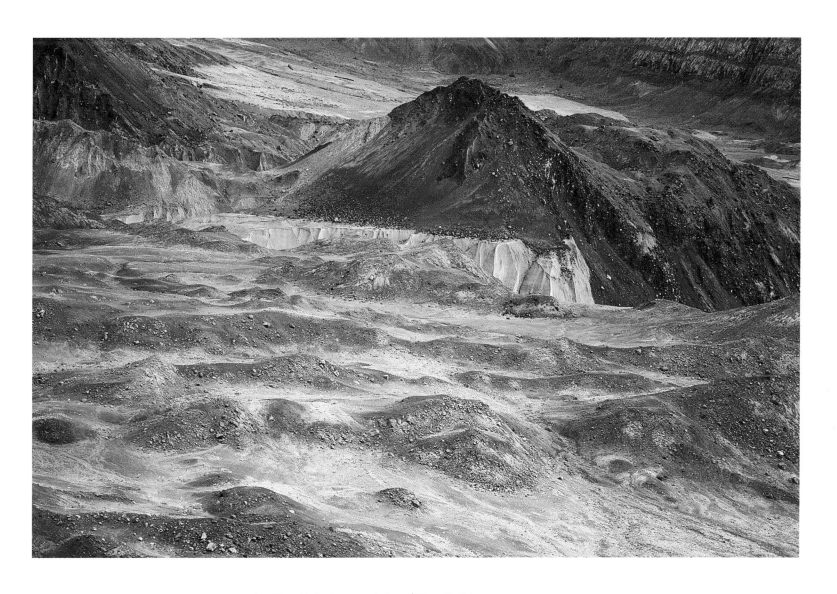

◄ and ▲ Unearthly landscapes at the base of Mount St. Helens.

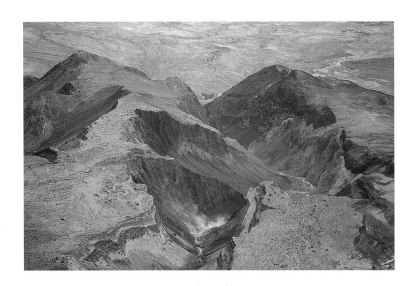

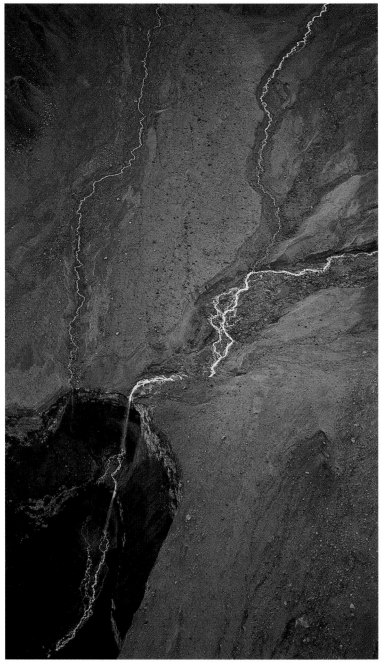

▲ Looking north from the eroded volcano lip to the pumice plain.

▶ and ▶▶ Dramatic waterfalls below the crater, formed by water action on the soft pumice, ash, and debris.

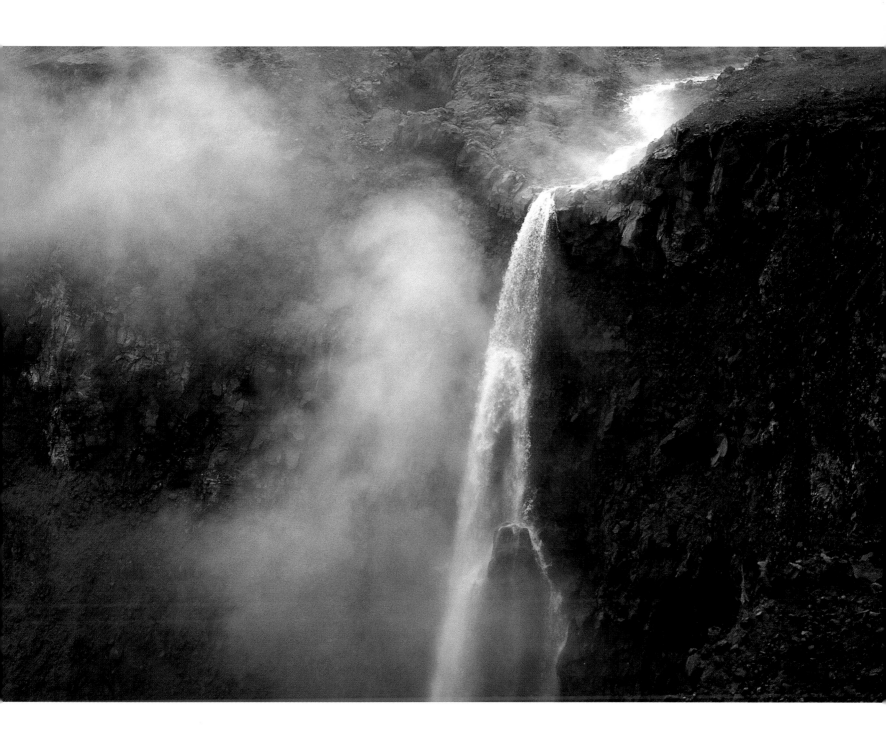

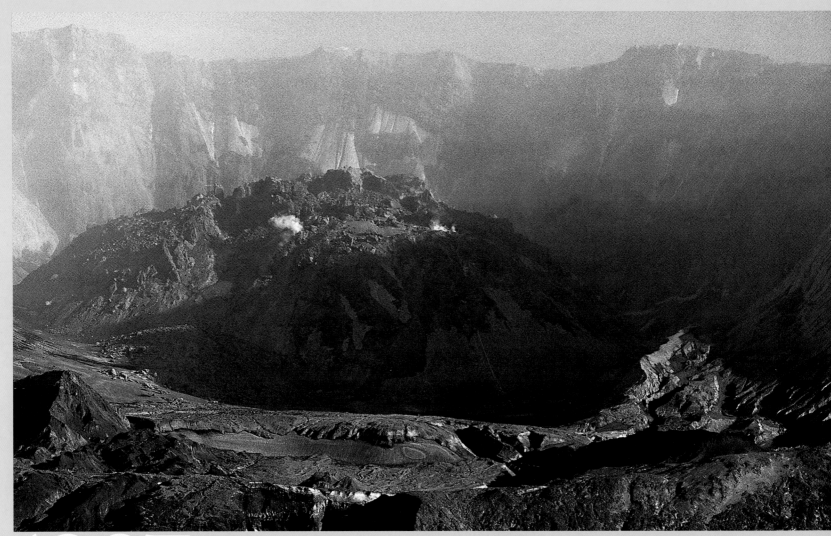

1987

▲ *A new dome made of successive layers of oozing lava, seen soon after dome building activity diminished in late 1986. Steam results from rain and snow seeping into cracks and then vaporizing when coming in contact with subsurface hot magma. On-going rock falls and wind create hazy dust inside the crater.*

▶ *Without hot emissions, snow can survive on the dome, which is three thousand feet across and nine hundred feet tall.*

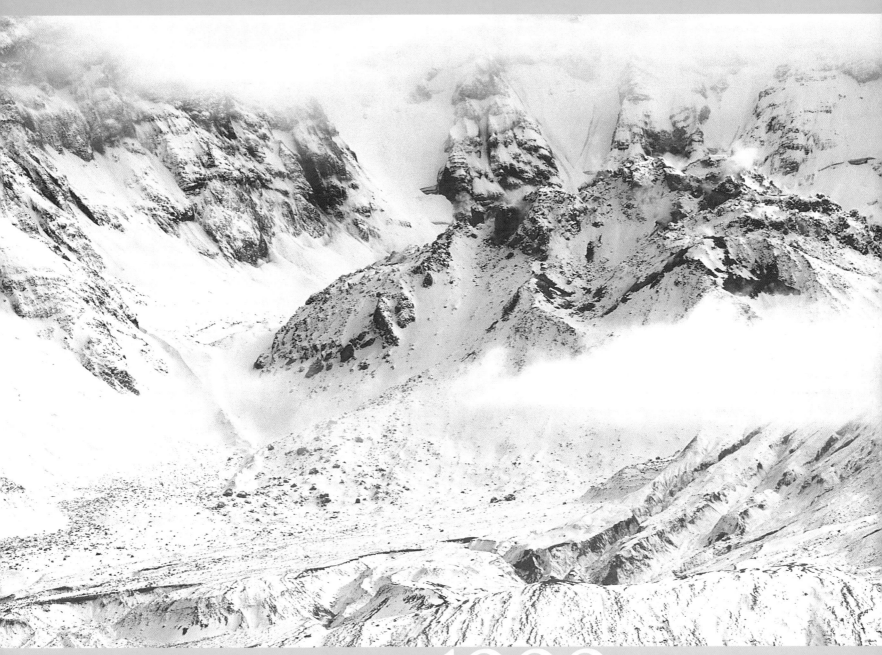

1999

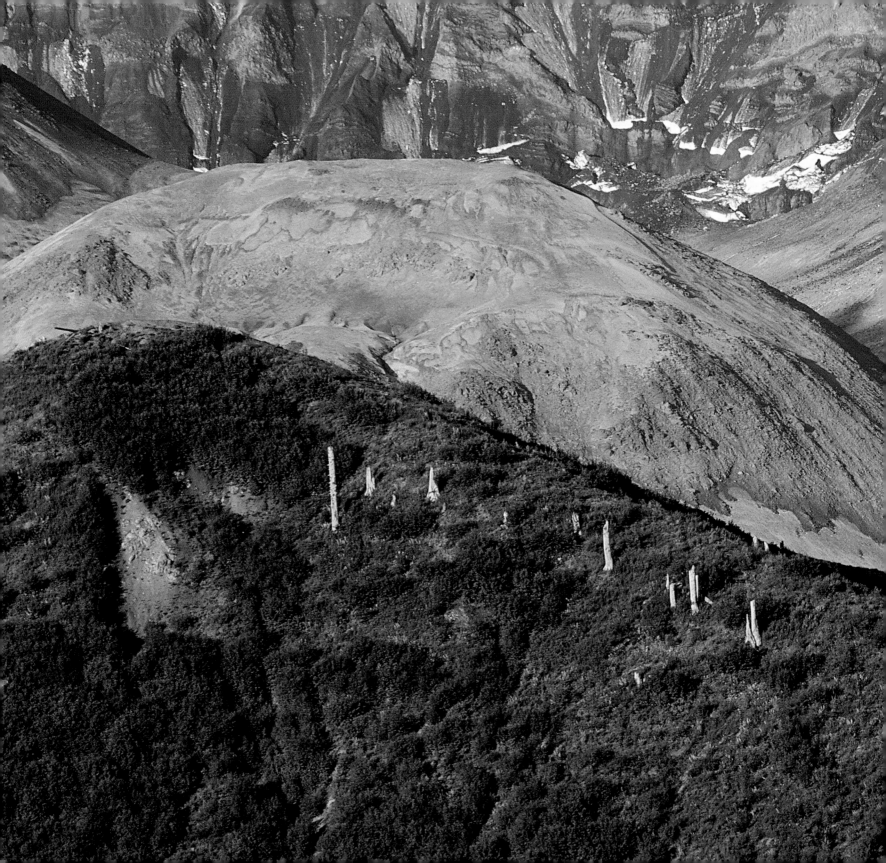

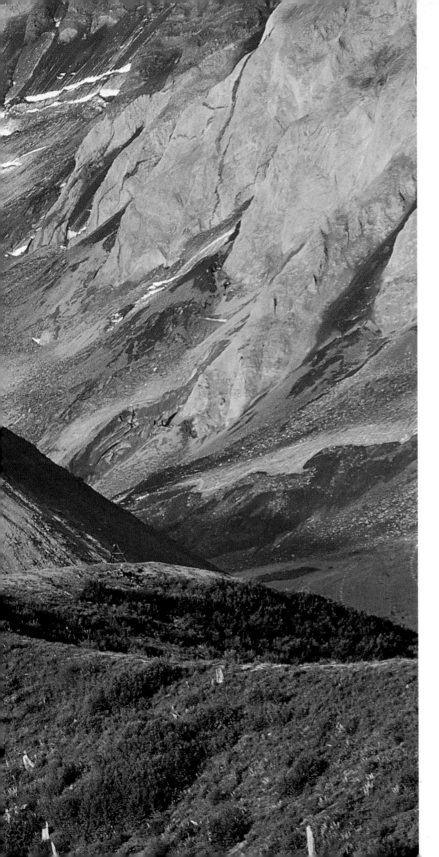

EAST
FROM WINDY RIDGE TO THE FRINGE

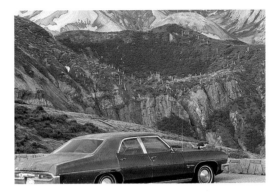

The east side of the mountain features log-covered Spirit Lake and readily accessible areas of the naturally evolving blowdown and dead standing zones within the Mount St. Helens National Volcanic Monument. The farther east one travels from the crater, the greater the presence of plant and animal life.

◄ Looking into the volcano from Windy Ridge. The mound is called Sugar Bowl, a thirteen-hundred-year-old lava dome.

▲ Several million visitors come to Mount St. Helens annually, some heading here to the end of Forest Service road 99, just four miles from the mountain. Up to one-fifth of visitors are from outside the United States, such as the owner of this well traveled car with Germany stickers and Texas style horns.

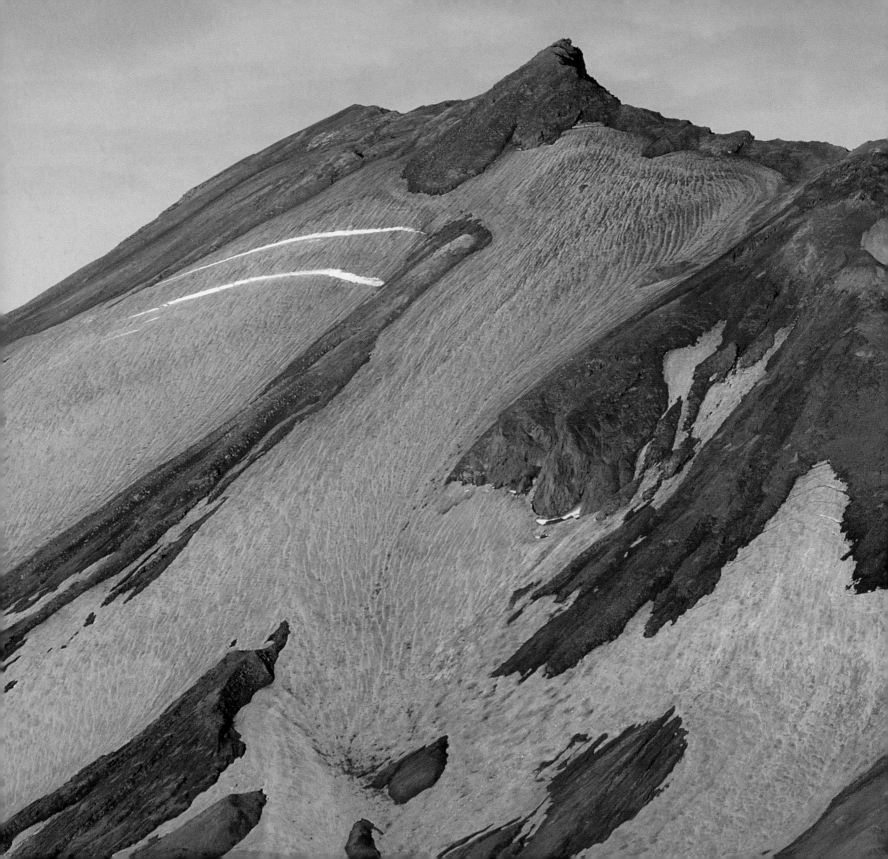

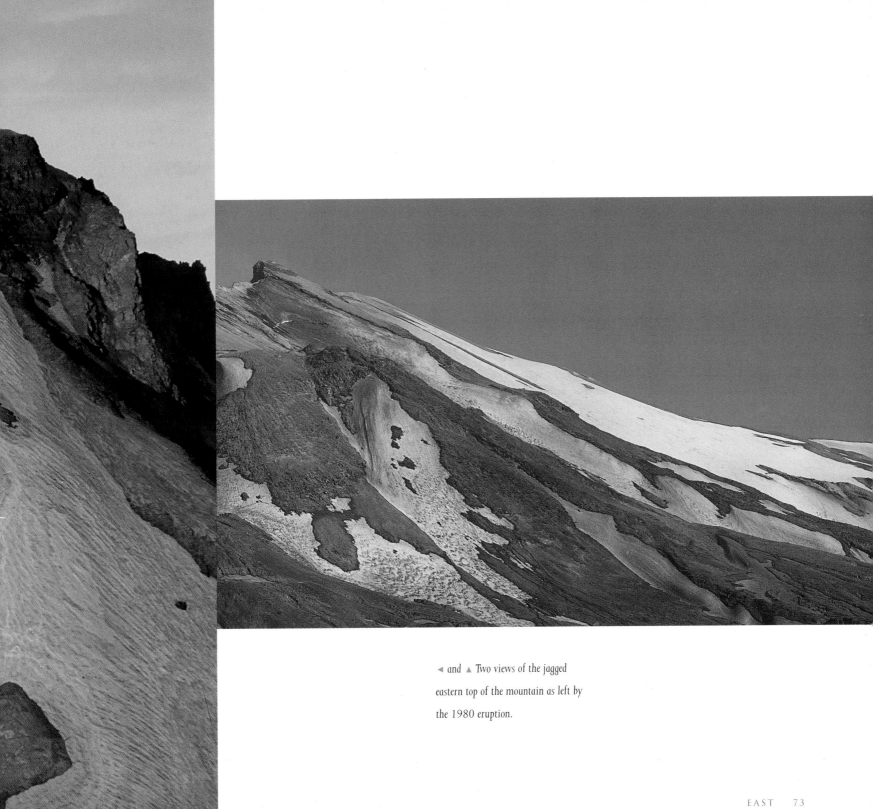

◄ and ▲ Two views of the jagged
eastern top of the mountain as left by
the 1980 eruption.

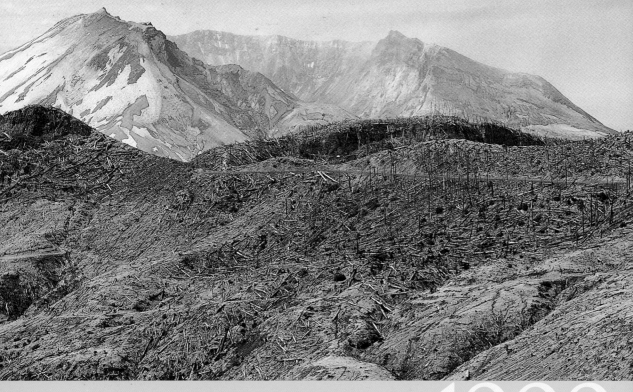

1987

1999

Mount St. Helens from the east.

▶ Before dawn.

▲ Twelve years earlier, with damage clearly evident
on the hillsides facing away from the volcano.

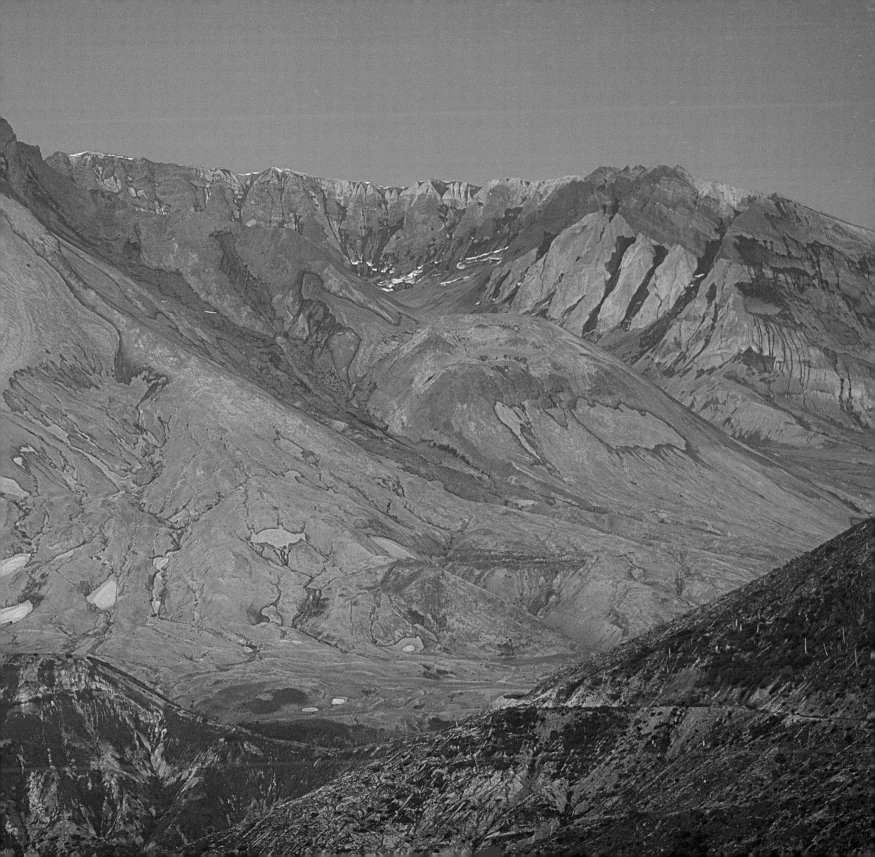

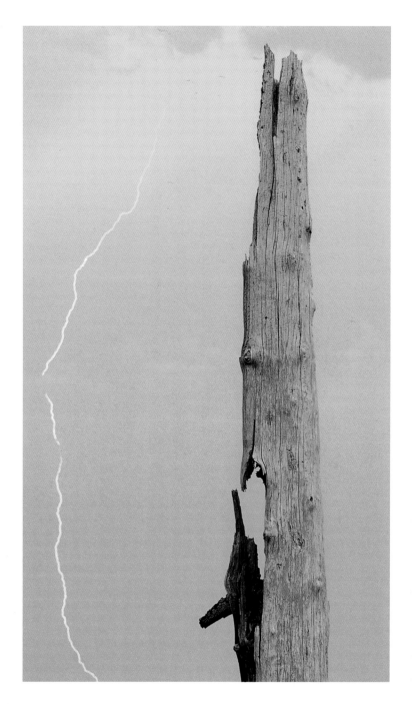

◄ Evening lightning seen near Smith Creek Trailhead, preceding a night of strikes all around the mountain. During the 1980 eruption, lightning induced by ash particles in the air started many forest fires, adding to the destruction.

► Sunshine above the clouds engulfing Smith Creek on the flanks of Mount St. Helens.

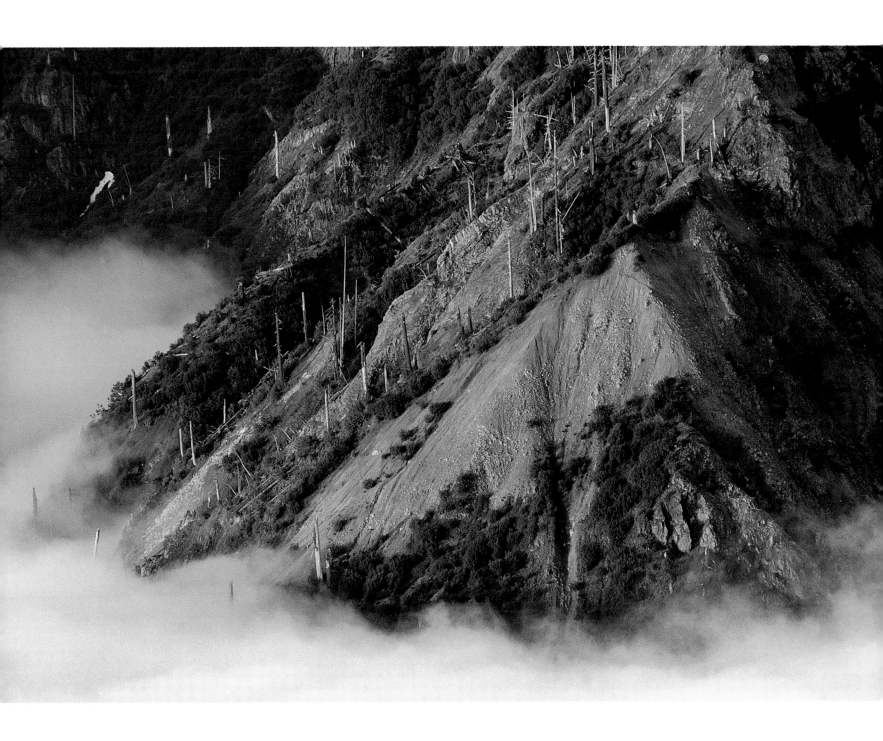

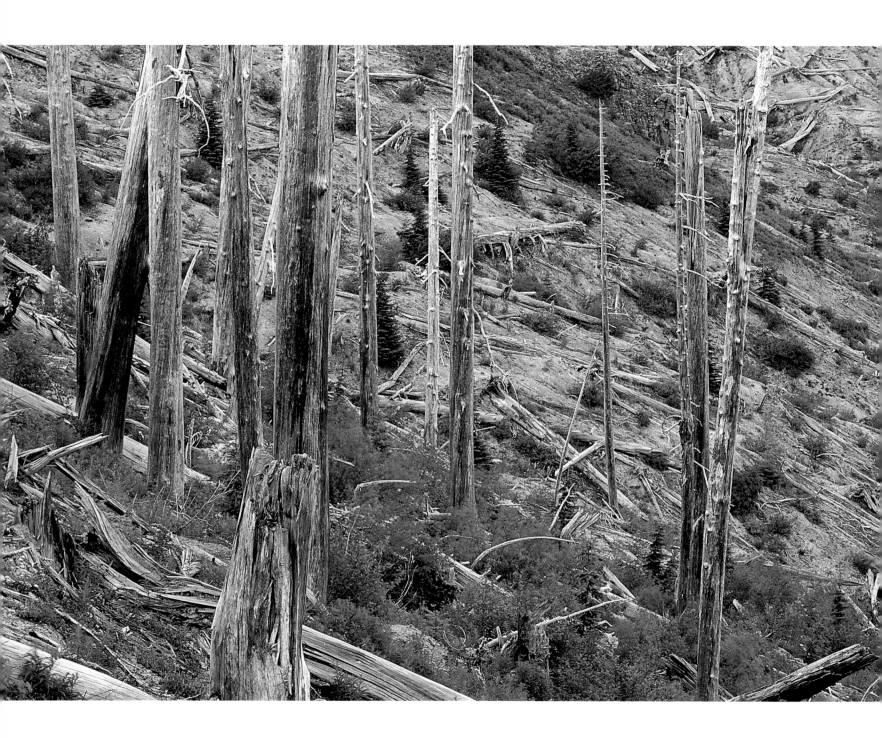

◄ Just below the east side of a ridge five miles from the mountain. Damage from the lateral explosion increases and new growth decreases from left to right as the protective effect of the ridge top diminishes.

► Broad leaf lupine near Spirit Lake, likely established from wind blown seed.

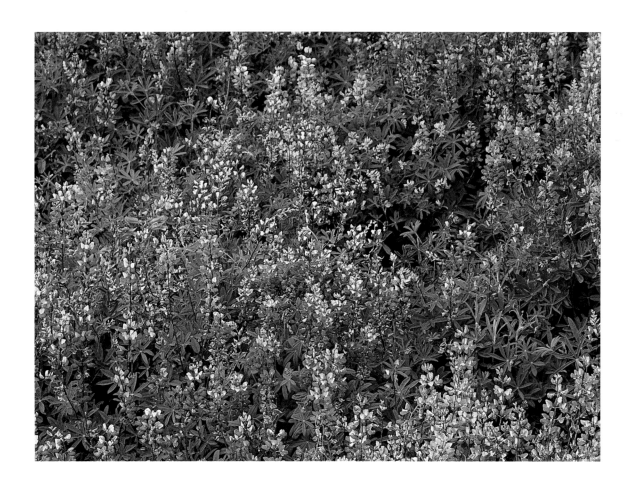

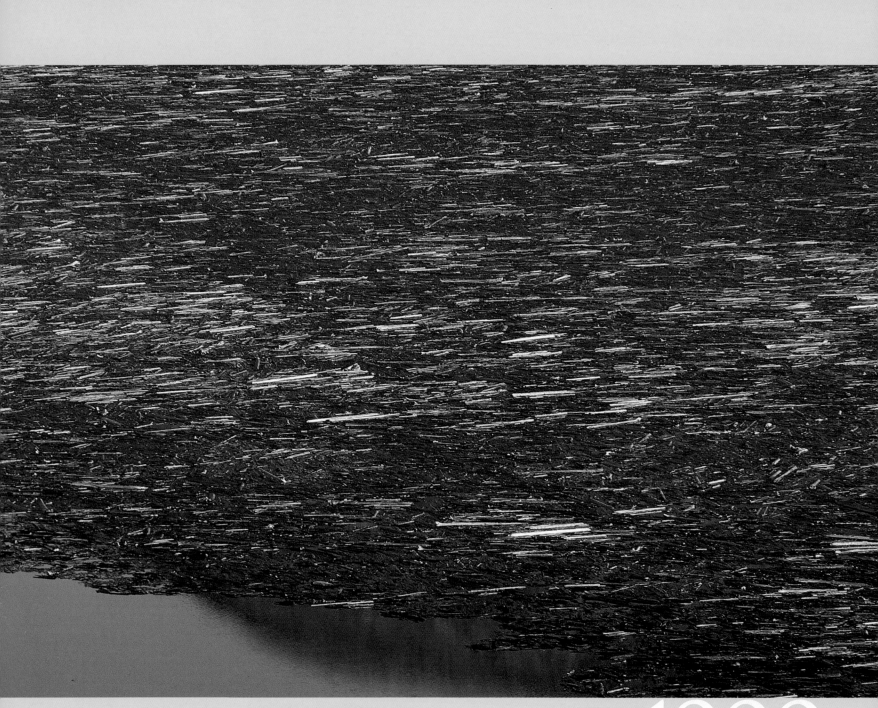

1999

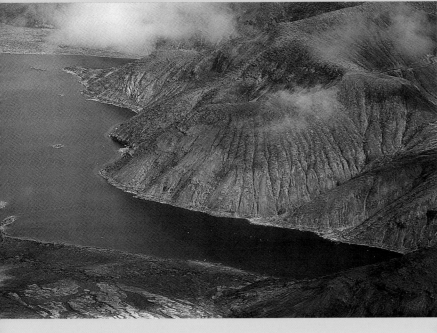

1989

1991

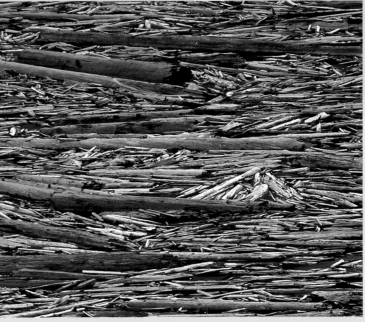

Spirit Lake and its shore-side hills suffered the effects of a two hundred foot high wave triggered when a portion of the eruption landslide plunged into the lake's western edge. The receding water of the giant wave pulled trees down into the lake, where tens of thousands remain today. Landslide material raised the lake bottom and Spirit Lake grew significantly in surface area.

▲ The surrounding slopes display the eruption's scouring effects. Forest Service road 99 is seen on the right. The public could drive a single lane here as early as the summer of 1983.

◄ Winds move the floating logs from one end of the lake to another, creating changing areas of open water.

► Tree chunks on the surface are large and densely spaced. Beneath the surface, the initially highly alkaline water has nearly returned to normal, and even with the log mat on top, can support life.

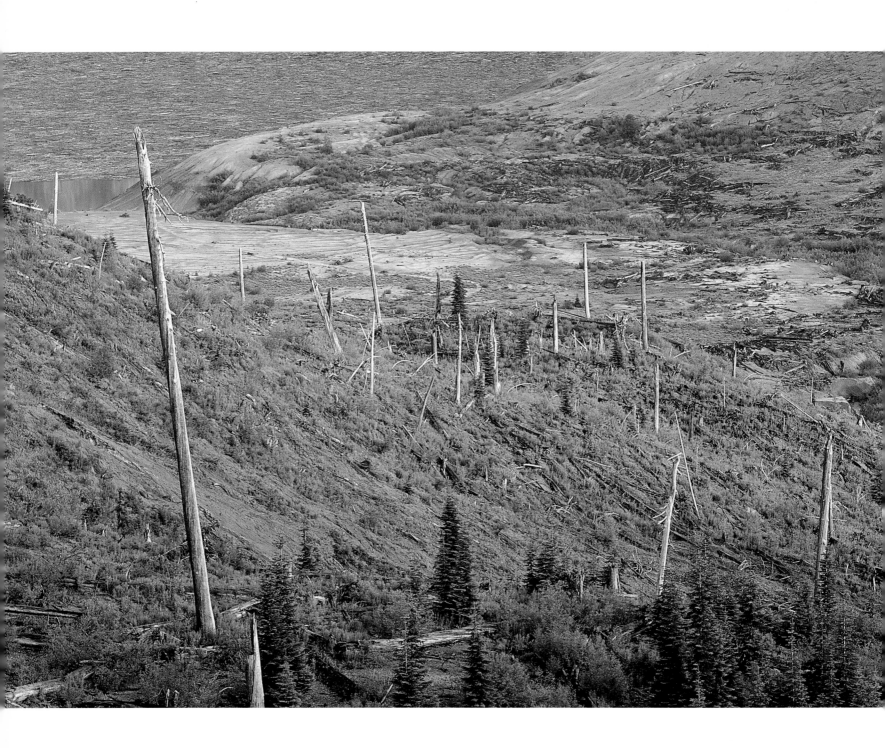

◄ Spirit Lake's northeast edge, where the arriving landslide-caused wave surged as high as eight hundred feet up the hills.

▼ A view of the inner blast zone near Spirit Lake.

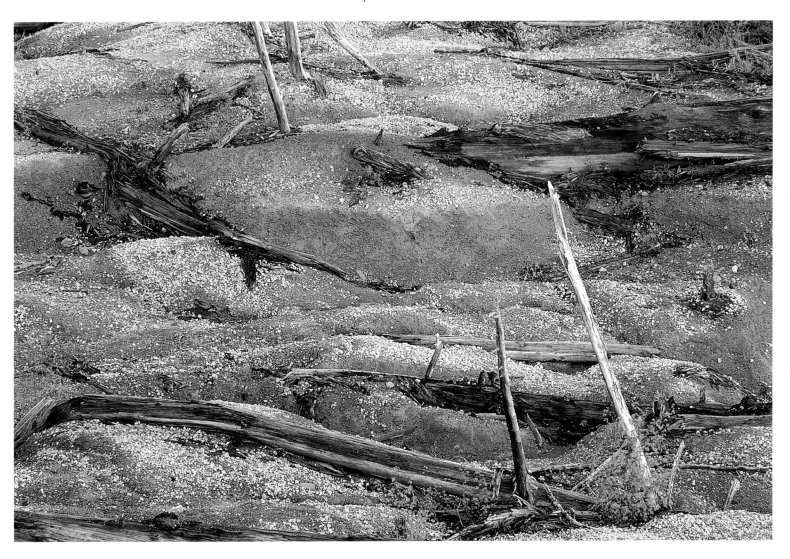

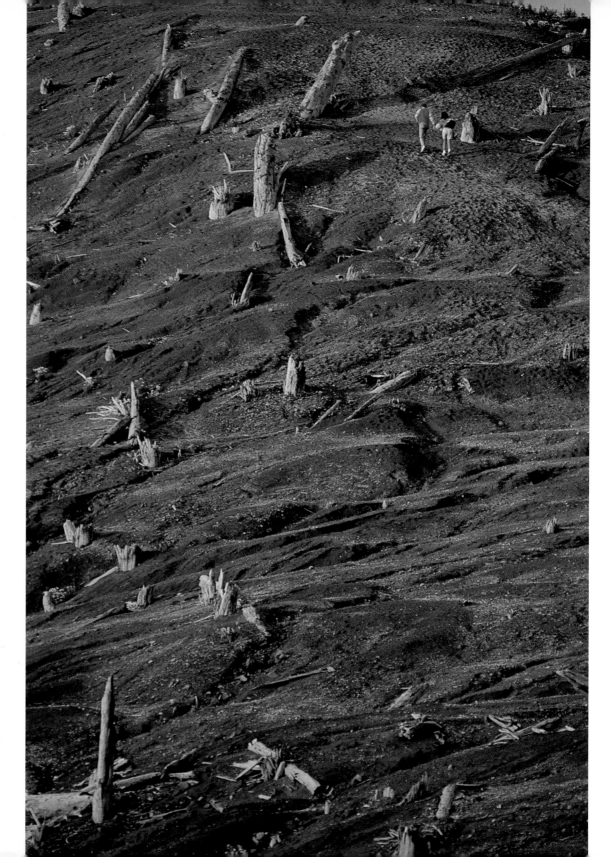

▶ Hikers in 1991 on the east side of the volcano. People were permitted back onto this side of the mountain well before they were able to travel along the Toutle River beyond the sediment dams.

▶▶ A section of the vast blowdown zone created by the lateral explosion.

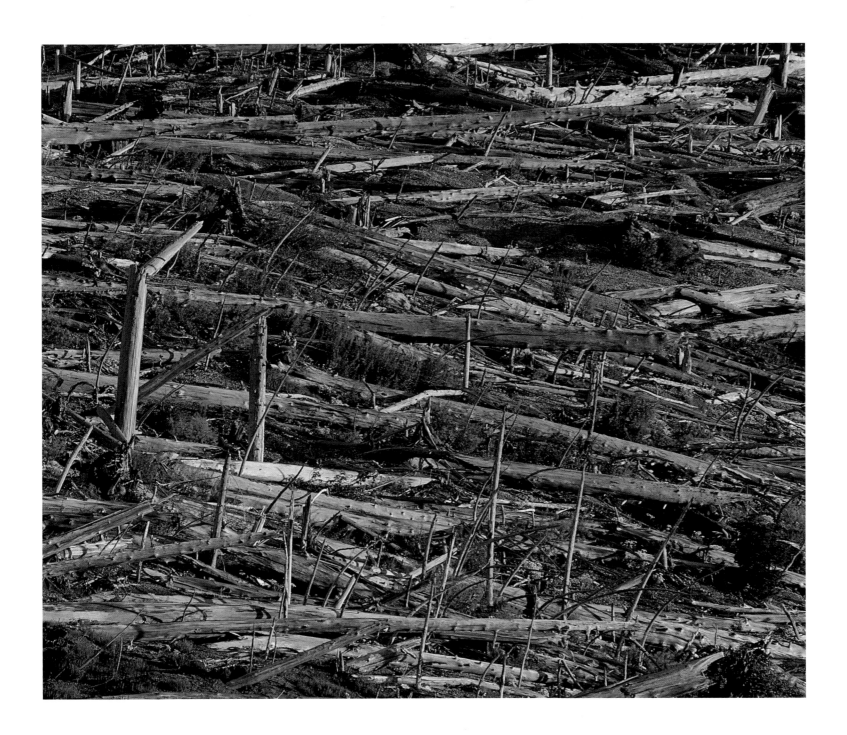

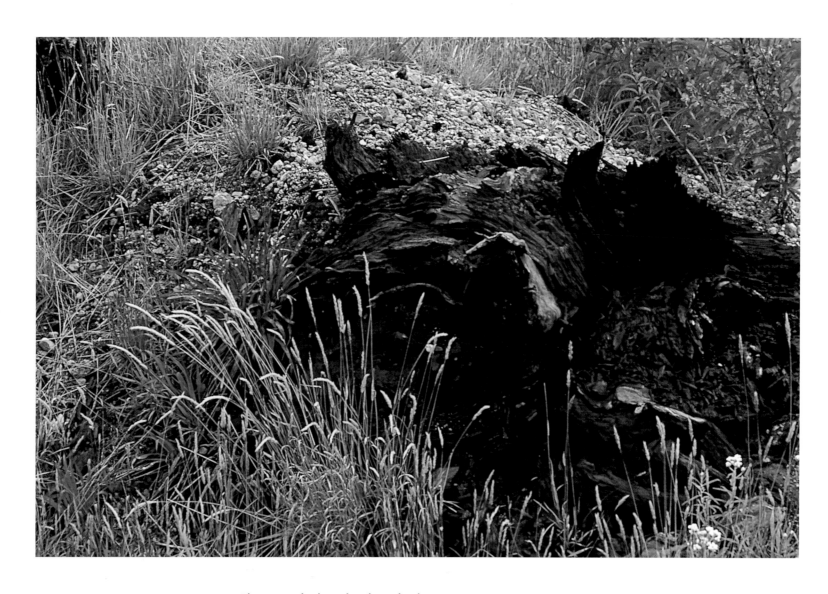

▲ Plants surround a shattered trunk topped with
pumice as nature hides the signs of the eruption.

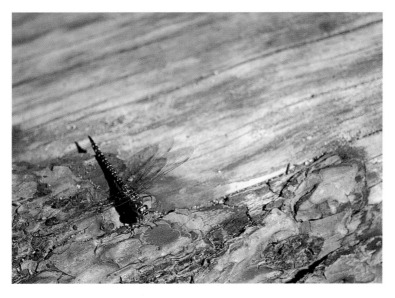

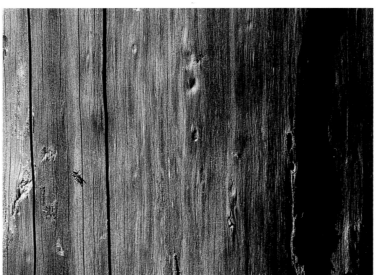

▲ and ◄ *A dragonfly (top) and a bee (bottom) rest on large trees felled by the lateral explosion. Because insects readily travel with the wind, they were among the earliest and most abundant recolonizers of affected areas.*

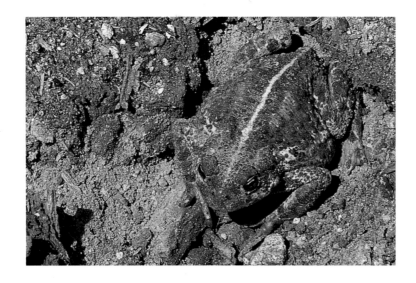

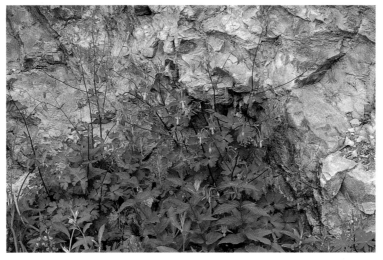

▲ A Western toad patiently awaits an insect meal in the blowdown zone. Many frogs and toads moved in, using their ability to travel long distances during cooler, wetter seasons.

◄ Red columbine takes hold. Flowers now provide splashes of color not seen in the dense pre-1980 forests.

► Tadpoles frolic in Meta Lake near the Volcanic Monument eastern boundary. Some amphibians survived the eruption by being under water that was covered with a protective layer of ice.

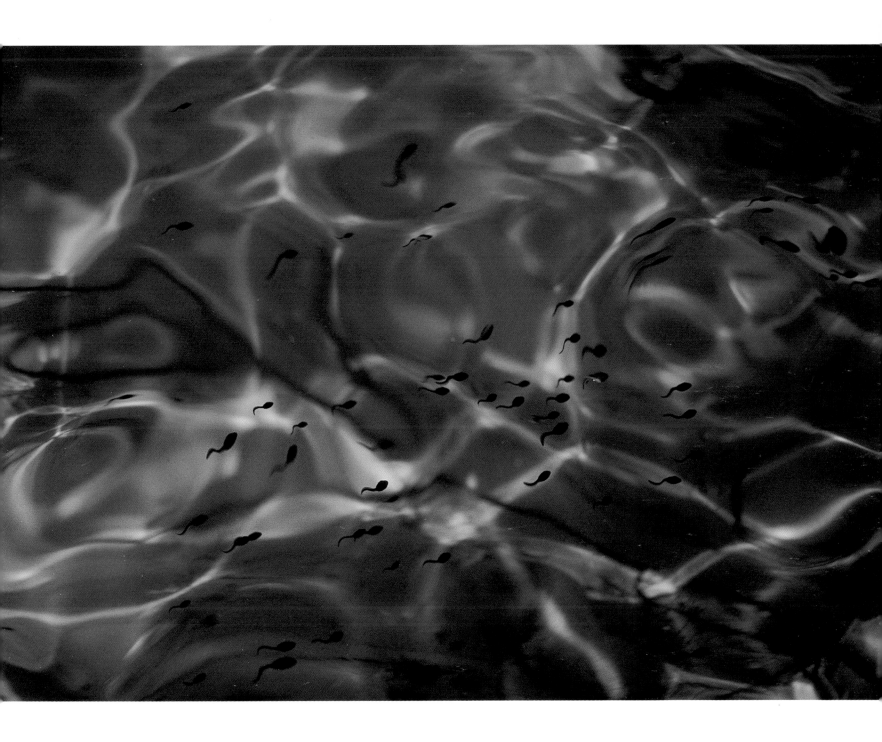

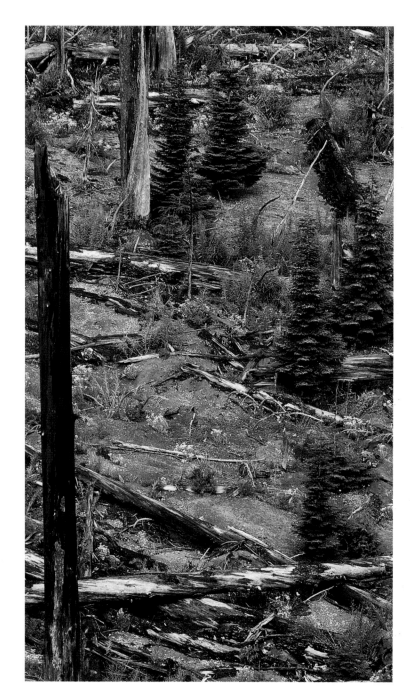

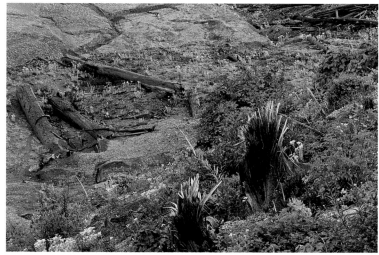

▲ The gradual outward spread of plant life is easily detectable in this scene.

◄ A mixture of old and new on the former forest floor.

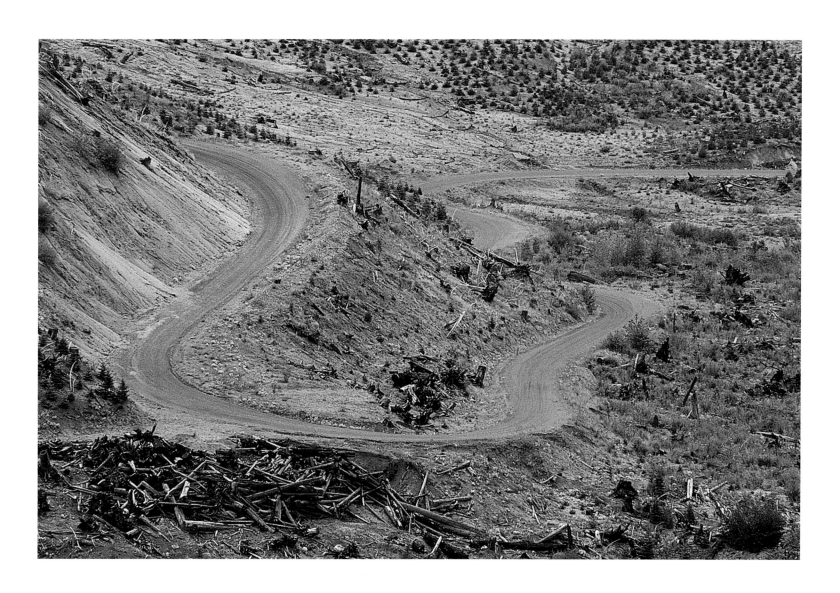

▲ *An area just outside the Volcanic Monument soon after replanting*
by the U.S. Forest Service. As of 1990, the Forest Service had planted
ten million trees on fourteen thousand National Forest acres, with fully
seventy percent of the seedlings surviving these harsh conditions.

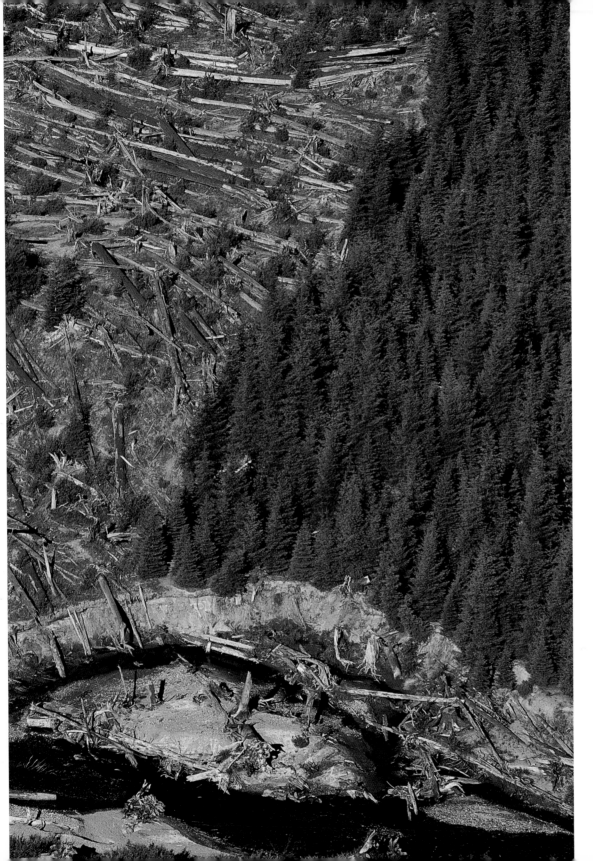

◄ The Mount St. Helens National Volcanic Monument boundary stands out as the sharp dividing line between the undisturbed blowdown area in the Monument on the left and the replanted area outside the Monument on the right.

► The standing dead zone of trees killed by the last gasps of the lateral explosion can be found along the outer edge of the blowdown zone, here ten miles from the volcano.

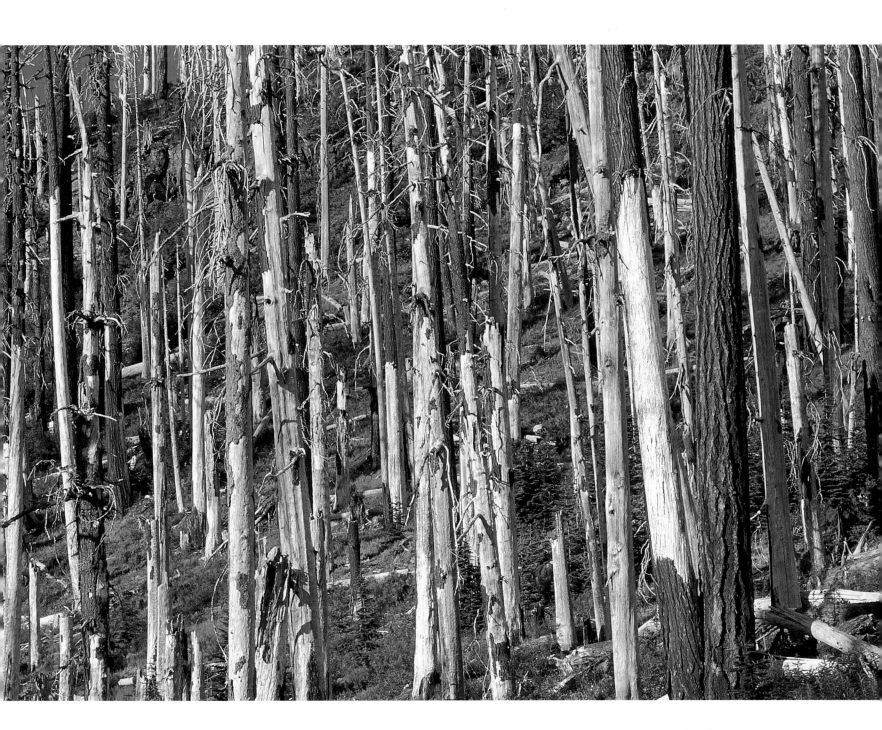

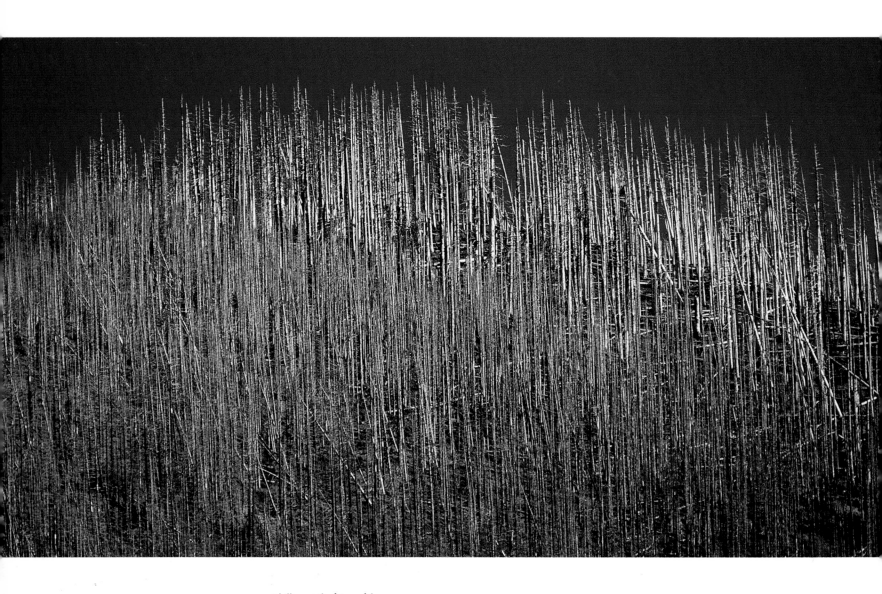

▲ *A hilltop at the fringe of damage.*

▶ *This forest is just beyond the reach of the lateral*
explosion and not far from the dead trees on the
two preceding pages. Much of the land near Mount
St. Helens looked like this before 1980.

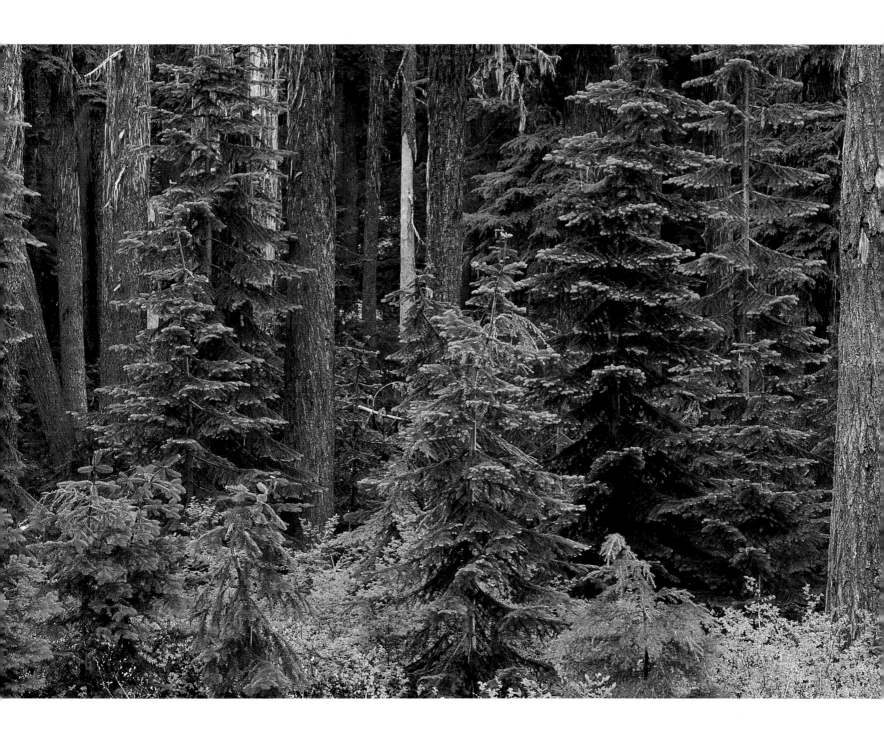

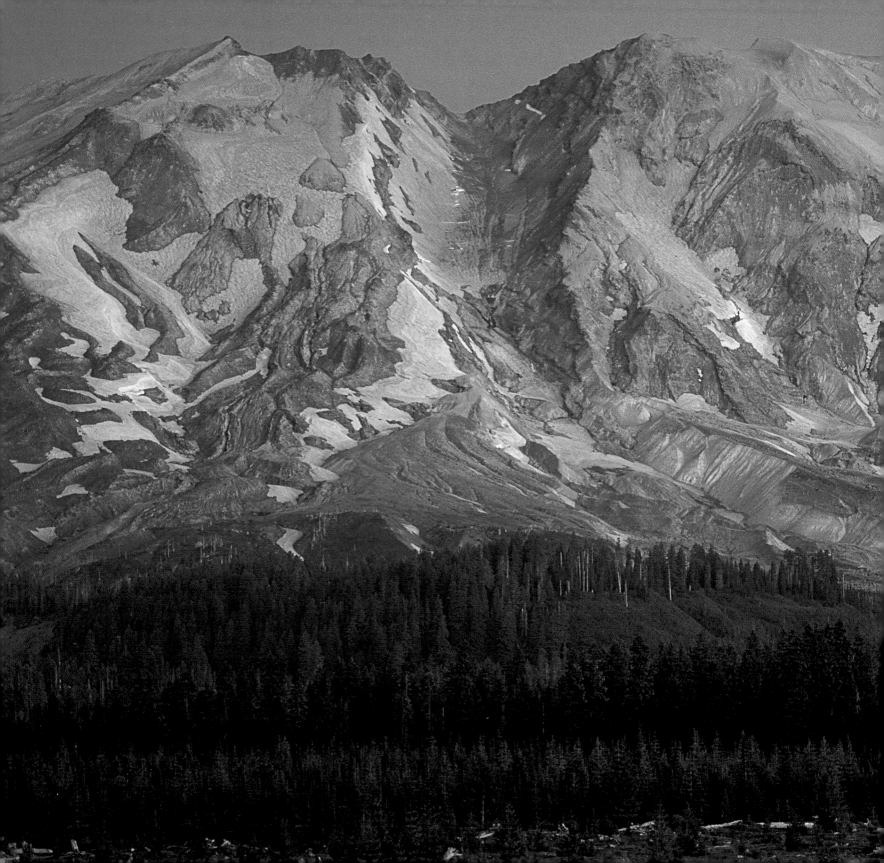

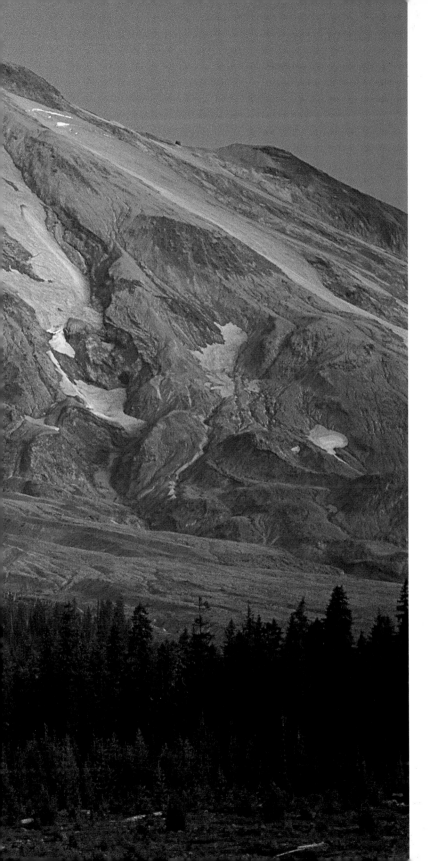

SOUTH
AROUND THE LAVA AND LAHAR

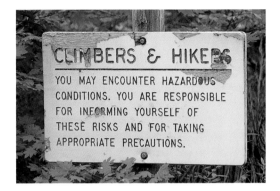

The south side of the mountain was least impacted by May, 1980, events, with the greatest damage associated with the impressive Muddy River lahar. As a result, this side reveals signs of both ancient and recent volcanic activity

◄ The large notch on the southeast face of Mount St. Helens is all that remains of the upper Shoestring Glacier. It lost three-fourths of its volume in the 1980 eruption when the top of the mountain disappeared and the glacier's snowfield melted, fueling a large mudflow.

▲ Warning sign for adventurers headed toward the volcano. Climbing was allowed again in 1987 from the south side of the mountain and over fifteen thousand annually attempt the seven to twelve hour summit roundtrip .

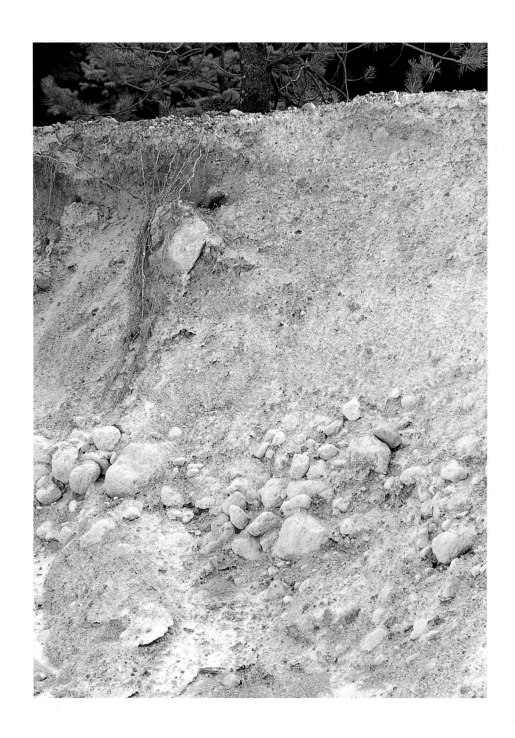

◄ Roots penetrate the pumice and ash collected beside Forest Service road 81. Over five hundred million tons of ash were deposited by the May 18, 1980, eruption.

▲ Lava casts were formed seven miles south of the summit nearly two thousand years ago when hot lava flows surrounded and killed large standing trees.

► A ladder allows visitors to descend into a lava cast on the Trail of Two Forests near Ape Cave. The bottom of the cast was ground level before the old lava flow.

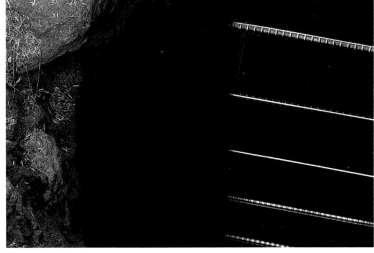

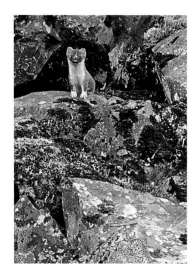

►► *A large lava field near Red Rock Pass left by a previous eruption.*

▲ *This short-tailed weasel surveys its stark territory.*

► *The rocks that give Red Rock Pass its name.*

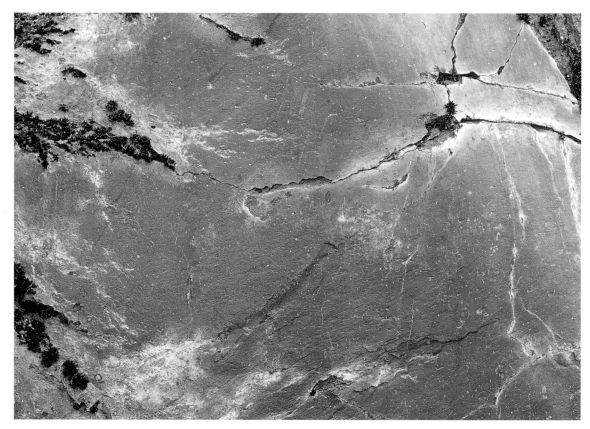

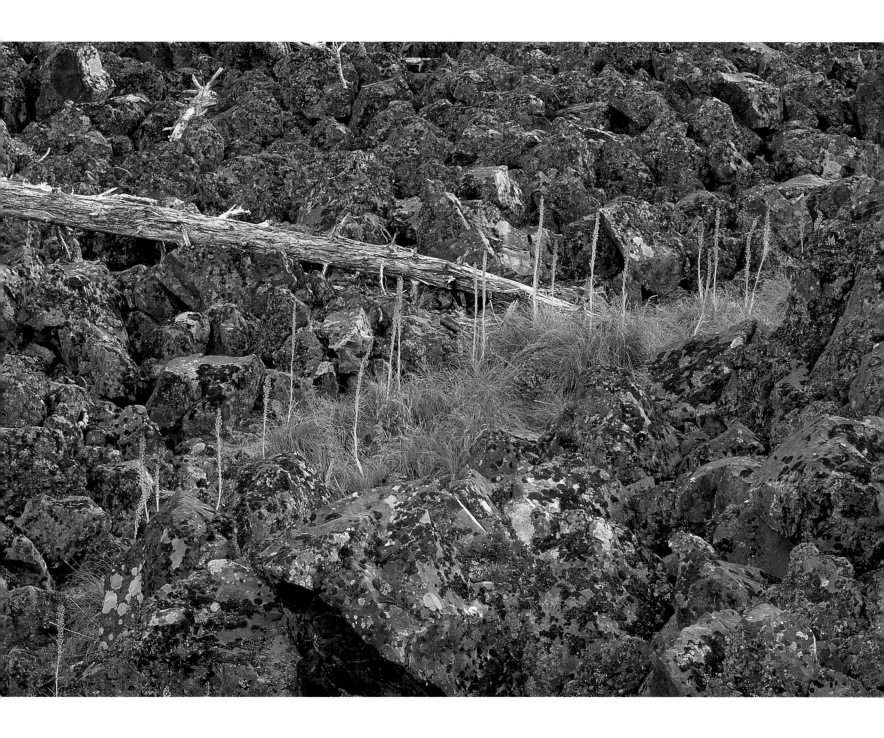

▶ The Muddy River flowing through Lava Canyon. Over the eons, the river has ground its way through volcanic deposits from numerous eruptions, including the 1980 mudflow that filled the canyon. The bridge is for hikers on the Lava Canyon Trail.

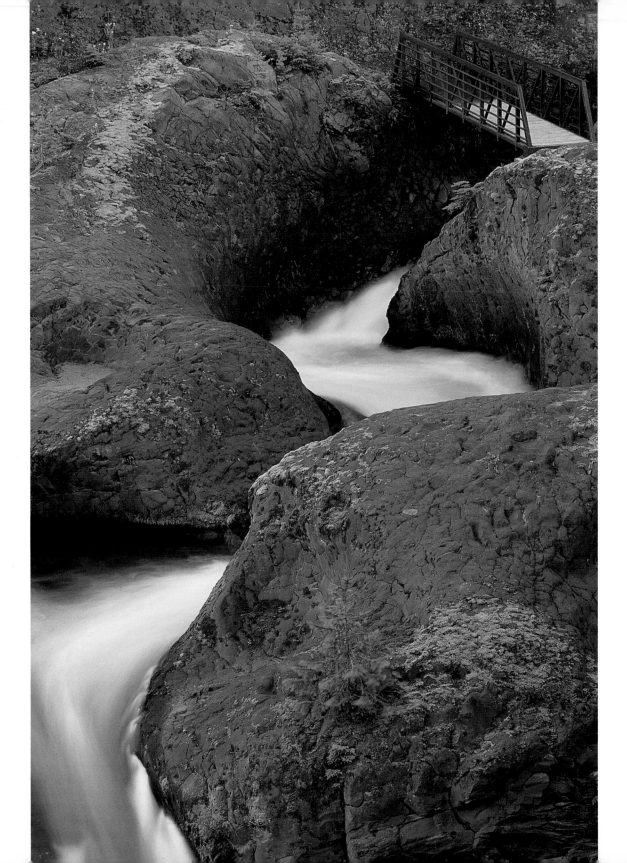

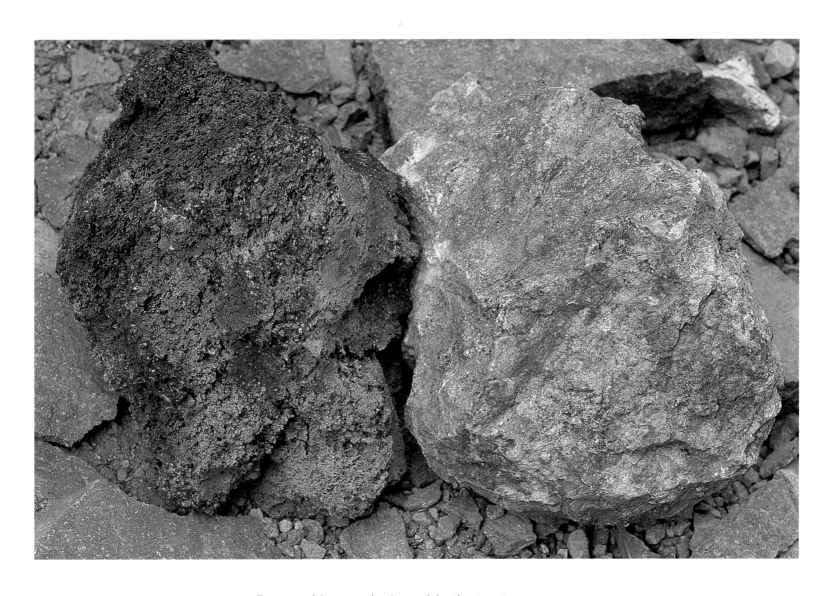

▲ Different types of the mountain's rocks rest side by side in Lava Canyon.

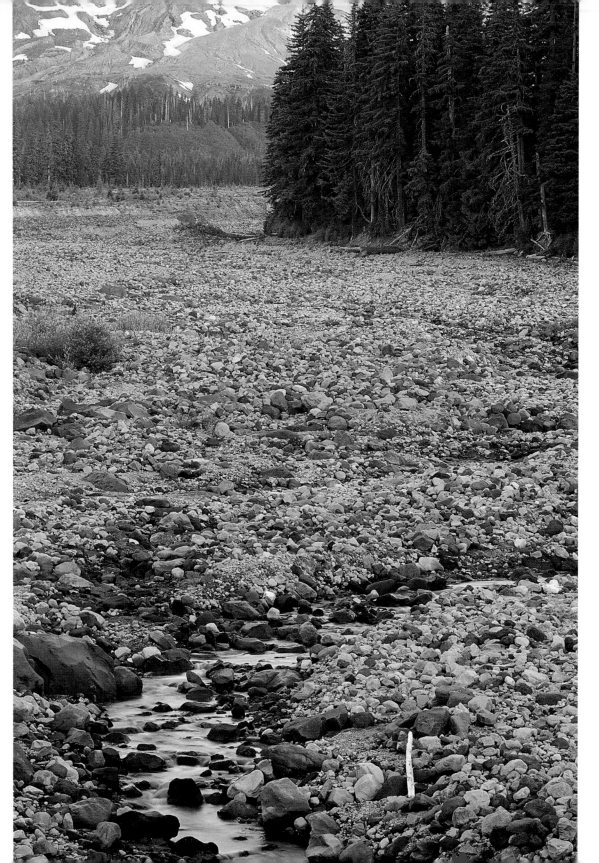

Melted snow and ice rushing down the mountain on May 18, 1980, from the Shoestring Glacier created a massive mudflow or lahar that overflowed the banks of the Muddy River.

◄ The lahar reached the location at the foot of this photograph in fifteen minutes, moving at over forty miles per hour.

► Layers in the Muddy River bank reveal deposits of past lahars and pyroclastic flows, with the 1980 mudflow on top. Because the south side of the mountain was spared both the landslide and lateral blast, only trees captured by the mudflow were killed, while the forest beyond was left intact.

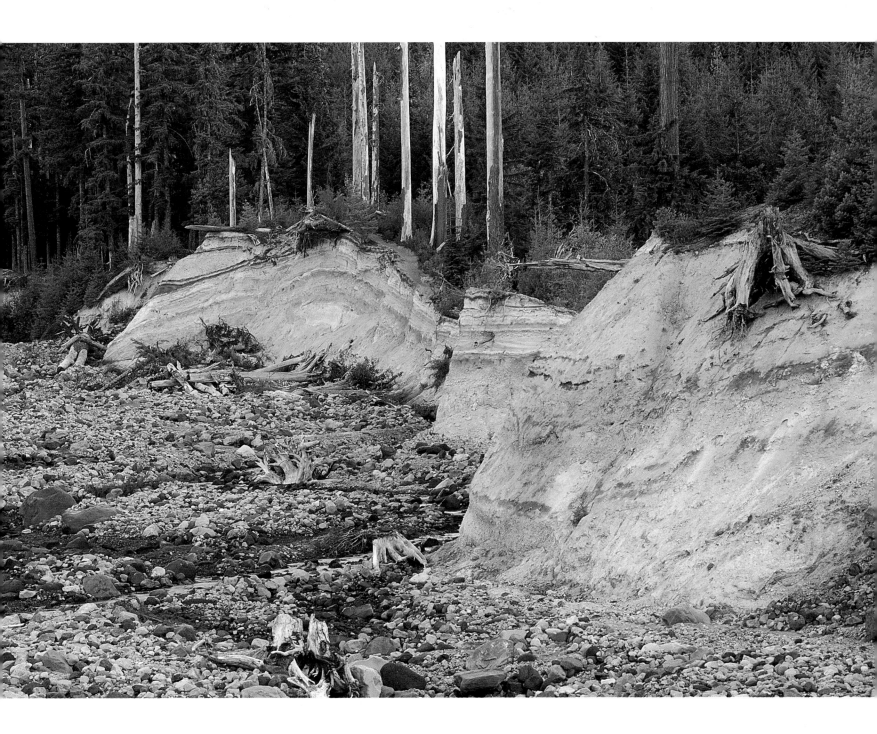

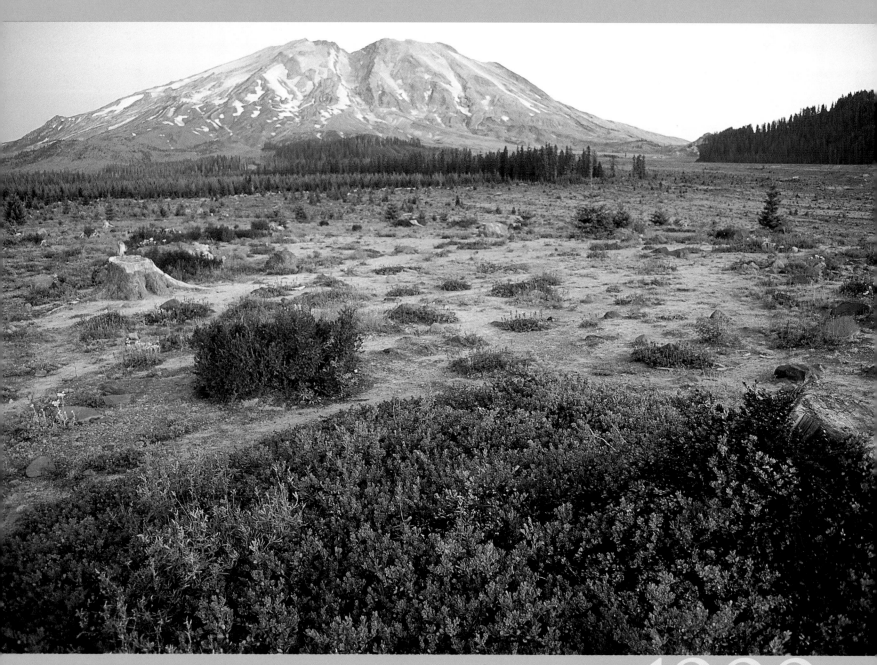

1999

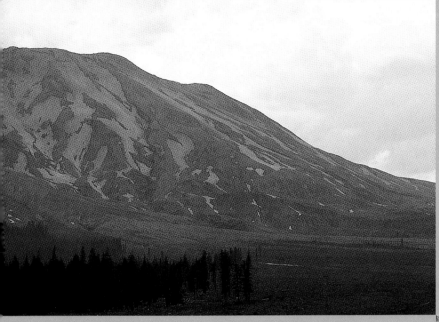

1999

1987

▲ The lahar split near where this photograph was taken, partly continuing down the Muddy River to the right and partly flowing into nearby Pine Creek to the left. The mudflow was powerful enough to take out bridges many miles further downstream.

◄ The lahar area recovered noticeably in the years between this view and the adjacent one. Vegetation fanning across the lahar develops both by spreading outward from small pockets of survival and from blown-in seeds.

► Rocks relocated by the volcano sit among newly established plants. The lush green at back reveals where a stream emerges that had been buried in 1980.

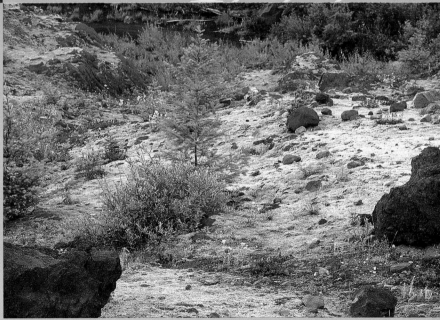

► *White-flowered pearly everlasting was one of the first plants to stake a claim in the aftermath of the eruption, often growing from surviving roots. Here on the edge of the mudflow, dense flora now stretches toward the base of the mountain.*

▼ *In 1987, a tiny seedling in the center of the lahar was a welcome sight.*

►► *A spot close to the seedling photographed in 1987, but twelve years later. The on-going process of renewal is apparent.*

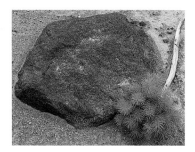

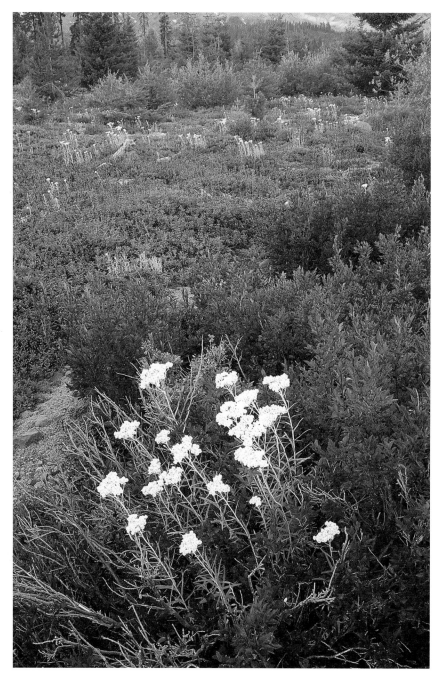

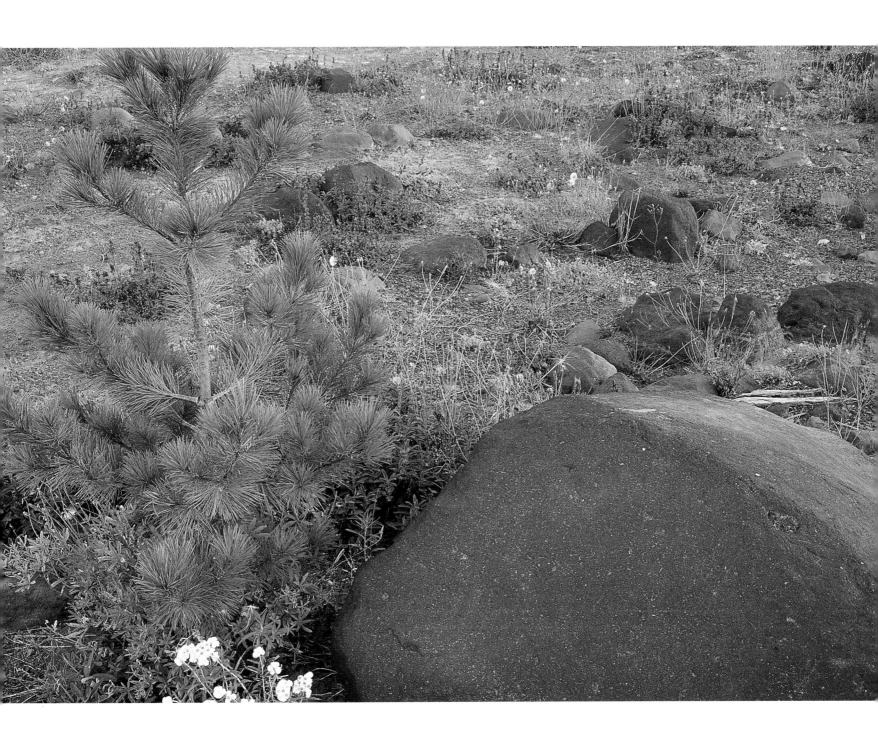

FOR FURTHER INFORMATION

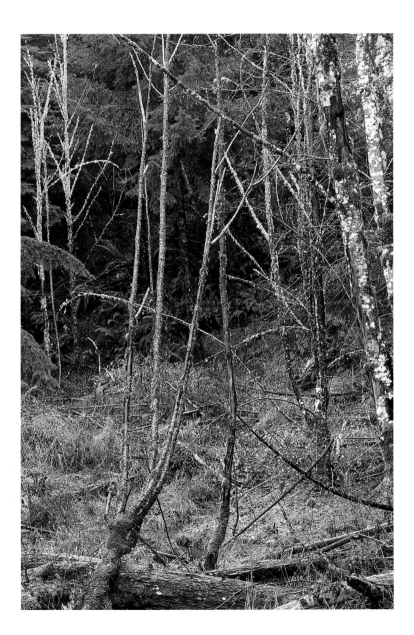

Michael P. Doukas, *Road Guide to Volcanic Deposits of Mount St. Helens and Vicinity,* U.S Geological Survey Bulletin 1859, 1990.

Mount St. Helens National Volcanic Monument internet site: http://www.fs.fed.us/gpnf/mshnvw/

P.T. Pringle, *Roadside Geology of Mount St. Helens National Volcanic Monument and Vicinity,* Washington State Department of Natural Resources Information Circular 88, 1993.

Robert I. Tilling, Lyn Topinka, and Donald A. Swanson, *Eruptions of Mount St. Helens: Past, Present, and Future,* U.S. Geological Survey Special Interest Publication, 1990.

U.S. Geological Survey Cascades Volcano Observatory internet site: http://vulcan.wr.usgs.gov/Volcanoes/MSH/

Klindt Vielbig, *A Complete Guide to Mount St. Helens National Volcanic Monument: For Hiking, Skiing, Climbing and Nature Viewing,* The Mountaineers, 1997.

◄ *A patch of forest near the old road to Spirit Lake.*

► *West wall of Mount St. Helens at sunset.*

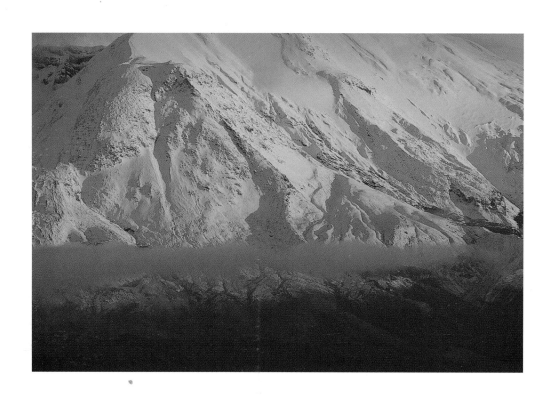